THE LITTLE BOOK OF
CHRISTIAN MYSTICISM

THE LITTLE BOOK OF
CHRISTIAN MYSTICISM

Essential Wisdom of Saints, Seers, and Sages

CARL McCOLMAN

HAMPTON ROADS

Cover design by Jim Warner
Cover art: St. Catherine of Alexandria, 1507-8,
Raphael (Raffaello Sanzio of Urbino) (1483-1520) © Bridgeman Images
Interior by Kathryn Sky-Peck
Typeset in Truesdell

Hampton Roads Publishing Company, Inc.
Charlottesville, VA 22906
Distributed by Red Wheel/Weiser, LLC
www.redwheelweiser.com
Sign up for our newsletter and special offers by going to
www.redwheelweiser.com/newsletter

ISBN: 978-1-57174-774-7

Library of Congress Control Number: 2017958284

Printed in Canada
MAR
10 9 8 7 6 5 4 3 2 1

CONTENTS

INTRODUCTION

I n the third and fourth centuries of the Christian era, spiritual seekers retreated into the deserts of Egypt, Palestine, and Syria to become hermits or monks, giving their lives to God in simplicity, austerity, and deep contemplative silence. They became known as the Desert Fathers and Mothers, and their wisdom and insight soon were committed to writing, to be passed down from generation to generation. Often in the desert, a younger person would turn to one of the elders for spiritual direction, encouragement, and instruction. The younger one would ask the elder for "a word"—usually a short, pithy sentence or two of instruction—which the younger one would retain for meditation and reflection; sometimes a hermit or a monk might devote weeks, if not months or years, to a single one of these "words" or sayings, in order to fully comprehend the richness of its wisdom.

From that time on, the inner tradition of Christianity, like other wisdom paths, has been passed down from teacher to student, generation after generation. From the Desert Fathers and Mothers to the monks and nuns of the great medieval cloisters, down to our time when increasing numbers of Christian contemplatives live not in monasteries but in the thick of our noisy, fast-paced society, acolytes of the mystical life have relied on the wisdom of our elders to inspire us, to challenge us, and to show us the way.

The wisdom of the Christian mystics is guidance for living in the love of God. God does not merely love us lavishly and joyfully, like a mother loves her child. Yes, of course, God does that, although thanks to centuries of religious misguidance, many people are blind even to this basic spiritual truth. But the mystics remind us that it gets even better than being loved unconditionally: the heart of the mystery is not just *being loved*, but *being love*. "God is not elsewhere," as a friend of mine once proclaimed in his blog. Or as Meister Eckhart part it, "The eye with which I see God is exactly the same eye with which God sees me. My eye and God's eye are one eye, one seeing, one knowledge and one love."

To be a mystic is to be a person of one seeing, one knowledge, and one love. *The Little Book of Christian Mysticism* gathers together an assortment of quotations from these visionary contemplatives, to invite you into their unique way of seeing, knowing, and loving.

As you will see, Christian mysticism is not linear. Think of it more as a spiral or, perhaps, a helix than as a line. Whatever progress it makes is marked by twists and turns, cycles and meanderings.

Unlike mysticism, however, books *are* linear. They arrange their content either as scrolls (ebooks) or pages (print books). Therefore, a collection of quotations like this could leave the false impression that mysticism offers a neat and tidy "program" for receiving, or achieving, union with God. That the point of mysticism is to reach the end as quickly and efficiently as possible. Answer the call, repent of the sins, cleanse the impurities, bask in the light, persevere through the darkness, and then enjoy the beauty of communion.

But that's not how it works at all (or more accurately, that's not how it *plays* at all). You could as easily start this book at the back, and move forward, and you would have just as meaningful and enlightening a journey through the wisdom of the mystics as if you began at page one. Pick up this book and open it up to any location, any page, and read. But don't just read: reflect, meditate, contemplate, *pray*. You've entered the circle. If something doesn't make sense, you might find an earlier quotation—or a later one—that clears matters up for you. Or not. That's just how the mystics roll.

This is the third book of a trilogy on Christian mysticism that I have had the privilege to create. If you're not sure what Christian mysticism is, then read *The Big Book of Christian Mysticism* (although "not knowing" about Christian mysticism is, arguably, an advantage). For more insight into the mystics themselves, consult *Christian Mystics: 108 Seers, Sages, and Saints*. Finally comes this little book, in which the mystics speak for themselves, without commentary or context.

Rather than trying to provide a comprehensive overview of mystical wisdom—as if that were even possible—the goal of this little book is more akin to the koan or the haiku: to invite you into the contemplative consciousness of the mystics through short, pithy quotations, intended to engage your intuitive heart rather than your discursive mind.

Antoine de Saint-Exupéry wrote about how to go about building a ship. The trick, he said, lies not in hammering nails into the hull or weaving canvas for the sails. Rather, the key to crafting a boat is to give the shipbuilders a taste of the sea. Likewise, there is no blueprint for the mystical life. If you want union with God, first you must have a taste of the open sea of silence and contemplation, where hints of the mystery of God might be discerned. Your heart will do the rest; and that largely means resting in the Divine Heart.

Mystics are in the business of giving us that taste for the ocean of God's love. This book, likewise, has as its goal to give you a taste of the mystics. Hopefully, you will find herein the call of silence, the call of wonder, the call of mystery. But if none of that happens, perhaps at least you'll be inspired to pick up a book or two by one of the great mystics, and carry on with your own unique search.

This book is divided into thirty-three sections (akin to the structure of an early mystical classic, John Climacus's *The Ladder of Divine Ascent*). You could use this as a "page a day" devotional and get over a year's use from it. But there's nothing wrong with just reading it straight through or picking a page at random and just diving in. It's your book, now, so read it as you wish. But don't just read: reflect, meditate, contemplate, pray.

Perhaps you may be surprised at the number of Biblical passages included. We have become so used to reading the Bible as a religious text, filled with moral imperatives and theological assertions, that we miss how luminous a mystical text it is. Likewise, students of Christian mysticism can get so immersed in the writings of Julian of Norwich or John of the Cross that we miss just how much their writings are filled with scriptural quotations and allusions. So it has become one of my priorities to help reclaim the mystical heart of the Bible—and the Bible as the heart of Christian mysticism. Hopefully the quotations included in this book will help more people to make that connection.

So turn the page, and meet the mystics. Be careful, for what follows are words that change people's lives. Once you get a taste of the salty silence on that open sea, you will never be the same.

Part One

PURIFICATION

I.

Every heart shelters within it a place of infinite longing. The German word for this is *sehnsucht*—which suggests a longing that is painful yet beautiful, so lovely that the ache of the yearning is itself a fulfillment. Alas, we live in such a noisy world, clanging with the chaos of our distracted minds and restless passions, so we often remain oblivious to our deepest yearning. Yet when we slow down and silence ourselves enough to recognize this desire for something that we cannot put into words, life will never be the same. We will follow that silent whisper in our hearts forever.

As a deer longs for flowing streams,
so my soul longs for you, O God.
My soul thirsts for God,
for the living God.
When shall I come and behold
the face of God?

PSALM 42:1-2[1]

The innate longings of the self for more life, more love, an ever greater or fuller experience, attains a complete realization in the lofty mystical state called union with God.

EVELYN UNDERHILL

Contemplate the hart of which David sings, weary with the chase, breathless, spent, plunging into the water, as though he would lose himself in its refreshing depths. Even so our heart, ever unsatisfied in this life in its infinite longings, rushes to God, its Living, satisfying Fount, in the next. There, as the famished babe cleaves to its mother's breast as though it would fain absorb it, so our panting soul cleaves to God as though to be for ever absorbed in Him, and He in us!

FRANCIS DE SALES

For our natural Will is to have God, and the Good will of God is to have us; and we may never cease from longing till we have Him in fullness of joy.

JULIAN OF NORWICH

To those who long for the presence of God, the thought of him is sweet, yet they are not satiated, but hunger ever more for him who will satisfy them, as he who is our food testifies of himself, saying, "they who eat me shall still hunger," and he who was fed said, "I will be satisfied when your glory appears."

BERNARD OF CLAIRVAUX

Let us consider our soul as a castle, composed entirely of diamonds, or very clear crystal, in which there are many rooms, just as in Heaven there are many mansions . . . I know of nothing to which I can compare the great beauty of a soul, and its wonderful capacity. Truly, however enlarged our understanding may be, it is unable to comprehend the beauty of a soul, just as it cannot comprehend who God is; for He saith Himself, that He created us to His own image and likeness.

TERESA OF ÁVILA

I am not now living in myself,

And without God I cannot live;

For without God, I am also without myself.

JOHN OF THE CROSS

When you were living like an ordinary Christian in the company of your worldly friends, the everlasting love of the Godhead, by which God made you and formed you when you were nothing, and then bought you with the price of His precious blood when you were lost in Adam, would not permit you to be so far from Him in form and degree of living. Therefore He kindled your desire full graciously, and fastened by it a leash of longing, and led you by it into a more special state and form of living, to be a servant among God's special servants, where you might learn to live more specially and more ghostly in His service than you did, or might do, in your previous way of life. But even then, He would not leave you thus lightly, for the love of His heart which He always had for you. See how lovingly and graciously God has brought you to this singular way of life, where, in solitude, you may learn to lift up the foot of your love; and step towards that state and degree of living that is perfect.

ANONYMOUS (*THE CLOUD OF UNKNOWING*)[2]

You inspire us to delight in praising You; for You have created us for Yourself, and our heart is restless until it rests in You.

AUGUSTINE OF HIPPO

During the days of His life on earth, Mary's Divine Son spoke these words: "If you ask the Father anything in My Name, He will give it you." Therefore I am certain You will fulfill my longing. O my God, I know that the more You wish to bestow, the more You make us desire. In my heart I feel boundless desires, and I confidently beseech You to take possession of my soul.

THÉRÈSE OF LISIEUX

There are deeps in our consciousness which no private plumb line of our own can sound; there are heights in our moral conscience which no ladder of our human intelligence can scale; there are spiritual hungers, longings, yearnings, passions, which find no explanation in terms of our physical inheritance or of our outside world. We touch upon the coasts of a deeper universe, not yet explored or mapped, but no less real and certain than this one in which our mortal senses are at home. We cannot explain our normal selves or account for the best things we know—or even for our condemnation of our poorer, lower self—without an appeal to and acknowledgment of a divine Guest and Companion who is the real presence of our central being.

RUFUS JONES

II.

No one chooses to be a mystic. You may choose your profession, your interests, and your passions, but the mystical life is a calling, and we do not call ourselves. It is God's call. Of course, God has chosen you, for God calls everyone; in the words of a Carmelite friar, "the mystic is not a special kind of person; each person is a special kind of mystic." You are called to be the person God has created you to be, which may or may not line up with your own ideas. Nevertheless, we are all called to the possibility of deep intimacy with God, and even invited into profound union with God. All of us. So the question is, how will you answer your call?

But now thus says the Lord . . .
"Do not fear, for I have redeemed you;
I have called you by name, you are mine.
When you pass through the waters, I will be with you;
and through the rivers, they shall not overwhelm you;
when you walk through fire you shall not be burned,
and the flame shall not consume you."

ISAIAH 43:1-2

The homeward journey of our spirit, then, may be thought of as due to the push of a divine life within, answering to the pull of a divine life without. It is only possible because there is already in that spirit a certain kinship with the Divine, a capacity for Eternal Life; and the mystics, in undertaking it, are humanity's pioneers on the only road to rest . . . The spiritual pilgrim goes because he is called; because he wants to go, must go, if he is to find rest and peace. "God needs man," says Eckhart. It is Love calling to love: and the journey, though in one sense a hard pilgrimage, up and out, by the terraced mount and the ten heavens to God, in another is the inevitable rush of the roving comet, caught at last, to the Central Sun. "My weight is my love," said St. Augustine. Like gravitation, it inevitably compels, for good or evil, every spirit to its own place. According to another range of symbols, that love flings open a door, in order that the larger Life may rush in, and it and the soul be "one thing."

EVELYN UNDERHILL

True devotion presupposes, not a partial, but a thorough love of God. For inasmuch as divine love adorns the soul, it is called grace, making us pleasing to the Divine Majesty: inasmuch as it gives us the strength to do good, it is called charity; but when it has arrived at that degree of perfection, by which it not only makes us act well, but also work diligently, frequently, and readily, then it is called devotion.

FRANCIS DE SALES

Suddenly the Trinity fulfilled my heart with most joy. And so I understood that in heaven it shall be, without end. For the Trinity is God, God is the Trinity. The Trinity is our maker, the Trinity is our keeper, the Trinity is our everlasting lover, the Trinity is our endless joy and our bliss, by our Lord Jesus Christ and in our Lord Jesus Christ.

JULIAN OF NORWICH

The Little Book of Christian Mysticism

If you would grasp Christ, you will do so sooner by following him than by reading of him . . . Believe me as one who has experience, you will find much more among the woods than ever you will among books. Woods and stones will teach you what you can never hear from any master.

BERNARD OF CLAIRVAUX

This Lord of ours is so anxious that we should desire Him and strive after His companionship that He calls us ceaselessly, time after time, to approach Him.

TERESA OF ÁVILA

Have an interior desire that God may give you all He knows to be needful for you, to His greater honor and glory.

Have a continual trust in God, esteeming in yourself and in your brethren that which He most esteems; namely, spiritual good.

The more God gives, the more He makes us desire; until He leaves us empty that He may fill us with His blessings.

So pleased is God with the soul hoping in Him, and looking to nothing else, that it may be truly said the more that soul hopes for, the more it obtains.

JOHN OF THE CROSS

When our Lord said to Mary, who personifies all sinners that are called to the contemplative life, "Your sins are forgiven," it was not because of her great sorrow, nor for her remembering of her sins, nor even for her meekness from the beholding of her wretched state. But why then? Surely because she loved much.

ANONYMOUS (THE CLOUD OF UNKNOWING)

The Sun is but a little spark of His infinite love: the Sea is but one drop of His goodness. But what flames of love ought that spark to kindle in your soul: what seas of affection ought to flow for that drop in your bosom! The heavens are the canopy, and the earth is the footstool of your throne: who reign in communion with God: or at least are called so to do. How lively should His divine goodness appear unto you; how continually should it rest upon you; how deeply should it be impressed in you! Verily its impressions ought to be so deep, as to be always remaining, always felt, always admired, always seen and rejoiced in. You are never truly great till all the world is yours: and the goodness of your Donor so much your joy, that you think upon it all day long.

THOMAS TRAHERNE

Fill your lungs deeply with God so that you can breathe Christ into the world.

CARYLL HOUSELANDER

God does not call those who are worthy,
but those whom He will.

THÉRÈSE OF LISIEUX

And if you would know God be not therefore a solver of
    riddles.

Rather look about you and you shall see Him playing
    with your children.

    And look into space; you shall see Him walking in the
    cloud, outstretching His arms in the lightning and
    descending in rain.

You shall see Him smiling in flowers, then rising and
    waving His hands in trees.

KAHLIL GIBRAN

III.

It takes guts to embrace the mystical life. If we think of spirituality and mysticism as "nice" concerns of only those who are polite and well-mannered, then we haven't fully considered just how terrifying the encounter with the Divine can be. The Bible may promise us that the pure in heart will see God, but it also warns that no one may see the face of God and live. Even before we consider the world-shattering power of the mystical encounter, we know that people die for their faith every day. Can we expect any less? Contemplatives must embody the courage of a martyr's heart, never knowing when the time of trial may come—or what death may come to call us into a new, but very different, way of life.

For God did not give us a spirit of cowardice, but rather
a spirit of power and of love and of self-discipline.

II TIMOTHY 1:7

The Little Book of Christian Mysticism

More and more advancing in this inner life, the soul will feel the imperative attraction of Reality, of God; and it must respond to this attraction with all the courage and generosity of which it is capable. I am trying to use the simplest and the most general language, and to avoid emotional imagery: though it is here, in telling of this perpetually renewed act of self-giving and dedication, that spiritual writers most often have recourse to the language of the heart. It is indeed in a spirit of intensest and humble adoration that generous souls yield themselves to the drawing of that mysterious Beauty and unchanging Love, with all that it entails.

EVELYN UNDERHILL

There are two chief developments of our love towards God, one affective, the other effective ... By the first we give our affections to God and to that which He loves; by the second we serve Him, and obey His commands. The one unites us to His Goodness, the other causes us to fulfill His Will. The one inspires the love of complacence and benevolence, longings, and aspirations which tend to the union of our soul with God; the other fills us with the steadfast resolution, firm courage, and hearty obedience which are requisite to carry out God's Will, to suffer and accept willingly whatever it may be His Good Pleasure to send us.

FRANCIS DE SALES

We find meaning by abiding in God, faithfully trusting in God's mercy and grace. This is his own working in us, and of his goodness he opens the eye of our understanding—by which we have sight, sometimes more and sometimes less, according to our God-given ability to receive.

JULIAN OF NORWICH

I desire to serve only charity.

BERNARD OF CLAIRVAUX

It is of great importance, when we begin to practice prayer, not to let ourselves be frightened by our own thoughts.

TERESA OF ÁVILA

Everyone wants to receive the treasures and consolations of God; but very few are willing to enter into tribulations and sorrows for the Son of God.

JOHN OF THE CROSS

Lean meekly into the blind stirring of love in your heart. I do not mean your bodily heart, but rather your spiritual heart, which is to say, your will.

ANONYMOUS (*THE CLOUD OF UNKNOWING*)

The Little Book of Christian Mysticism

The very discovery of the nearness of God, of the sustaining power of His love, of the sufficiency of His grace, has come to men in all ages through pain, and suffering and loss. We always go for comfort to those who have passed through deeps of life and we may well trust Christ when He tells us that it is not the lotus-eater but the sufferer who is in the way of blessing and is forming the spirit of the Kingdom.

RUFUS JONES

The awareness of being a child of God tends to stabilize the ego and results in a new courage, fearlessness, and power. I have seen it happen again and again.

HOWARD THURMAN

He that sets himself to serve our Lord (especially in so high and divine an employment as contemplation) must prepare his soul for temptations greater and more unusual than formerly he had experience of; the which temptations will come from all coasts, both from without and within.

AUGUSTINE BAKER

IV.

Those who criticize the mystical life argue that it is a form of escapism, an attempt to avoid the gritty reality of embodied life. But that is not what the greatest mystics have taught. Far from rejecting reality, mystical wisdom urges a more authentic immersion into what is real: and that immersion begins with an honest encounter with one's own self. From the Buddha to the Oracle at Delphi, spiritual sages the world over proclaim, "know yourself." Christianity is no different. True, authentic self-knowledge leads to humility and mindfulness. It is also the mystic's path to God. Think of it this way: if we do not take strides to know ourselves, how can we ever know another—including the "ultimate" Other?

Examine yourselves to see whether you are living in the faith. Test yourselves. Do you not realize that Jesus Christ is in you?—unless, indeed, you fail to meet the test!

II CORINTHIANS 13:5

Few can bear to contemplate themselves face to face; for the vision is strange and terrible, and brings awe and contrition in its wake. The life of the seer is changed by it for ever.

Evelyn Underhill

Does not all such rousing and kindling of the soul to better things come of God? Is it not all done in and for us? We are roused, but we did not rouse ourselves; the Spirit of God roused us, and to this end it moved us. "I sleep, but my Heart (*i.e.* the Bridegroom) wakes," He calls me by His Love, and I know His Voice. God calls us suddenly, and as it were startles us.

Francis de Sales

God, of your goodness, give me yourself, for you are enough for me. I may ask nothing less that is fully to your worship, and if I do ask anything less, ever shall I be in want. Only in you I have all.

JULIAN OF NORWICH

Let not the creature, but the Creator be praised. Let Him who gives, not he who has received, be exalted: not he who plants nor he who waters are to be praised, for they are nothing, but He who gives the increase, that is God. I, then, will praise the hand which is stretched out to give, not that stretched out to receive: the praise of the Lord, and not of His servant shall come out of my mouth.

BERNARD OF CLAIRVAUX

If we can journey along a safe and level path, why should we want wings to fly? Rather, let's strive to make more progress in self-knowledge, for in my opinion we shall never completely know ourselves if we don't strive to know God.

TERESA OF ÁVILA

The first thing the soul must have in order to attain to the knowledge of God is the knowledge of itself.

JOHN OF THE CROSS

As long as the soul is one with the mortal body, no matter how sharp our understanding may be—in beholding of all spiritual things, but most specially of God—it is always muddied by some manner of fantasy; which leaves our spiritual practice unclean.

ANONYMOUS (THE CLOUD OF UNKNOWING)

At the center of our being is a point of nothingness which is untouched by sin and by illusion, a point of pure truth, a point or spark which belongs entirely to God, which is never at our disposal, from which God disposes of our lives, which is inaccessible to the fantasies of our own mind or the brutalities of our own will. This little point of nothingness and of absolute poverty is the pure glory of God in us ... It is like a pure diamond, blazing with the invisible light of heaven. It is in everybody...

THOMAS MERTON

Now the soul who wishes to rise above imperfection should await My Providence in the House of Self-Knowledge, with the light of faith, as did the disciples, who remained in the house in perseverance and in watching, and in humble and continual prayer, awaiting the coming of the Holy Spirit.

CATHERINE OF SIENA

The Little Book of Christian Mysticism

There is no one exclusive "way" either to the supreme realities or to the loftiest experiences of life. The "way" which we individuals select and proclaim as the only highway of the soul back to its true home turns out to be a revelation of our own private selves fully as much as it is a revelation of a *via sacra* to the one goal of all human striving. Life is a very rich and complex affair and it forever floods over and inundates any feature which we pick out as essential or as pivotal to its consummation. God so completely overarches all that is and He is so genuinely the fulfillment of all which appears incomplete and potential that we cannot conceivably insist that there shall be only one way of approach from the multiplicity of the life which we know to the infinite Being whom we seek.

RUFUS JONES

V.

Wake up! The joy of a new day begins with opening our eyes. Likewise, the joy of a spiritual awakening lies in our ability to open our eyes to the uncreated light of God's presence in our lives. It's tempting to see the point of the mystical way as having a sudden enlightenment experience—an immediate shift into expanded consciousness, heightened awareness of Divine union. But is such a sudden shift really what we want? Just as we prefer to wake up physically in a gradual, gentle, and unhurried way, the spiritual life may work best when it happens in a same slow manner. Take your time.

My beloved speaks and says to me:
"Arise, my love, my fair one,
and come away;
for now the winter is past,
the rain is over and gone.
The flowers appear on the earth;
the time of singing has come,
and the voice of the turtledove
is heard in our land.
The fig tree puts forth its figs,
and the vines are in blossom;
they give forth fragrance.
Arise, my love, my fair one,
and come away."

SONG OF SONGS 2:10-13

The Little Book of Christian Mysticism

You are not free. The awakening, then, of your deeper self, which knows not habit and desires nothing but free correspondence with the Real,-awakens you at once to the fact of a disharmony between the simple but inexorable longings and instincts of the buried spirit, now beginning to assert themselves in your hours of meditation—pushing out, as it were, towards the light—and the various changeful, but insistent longings and instincts of the surface-self. Between these two no peace is possible: they conflict at every turn.

EVELYN UNDERHILL

As the natural sunshine vivifies all things with its warmth, and with its universal love stimulates them to bring forth after their kind, so the sunshine of God's Love kindles every soul, and draws it to Himself . . . to live to God is to love; for he that loves not abides in death. How greatly then does God desire that we love Him! Nor does God stop short in thus generally calling us to love Him; yet more, He stands at the door of each human heart and knocks, promising that "if any one hear My Voice, and open the door, I will come in to him, and will dine with him"—in other words, God will admit him to the closest familiarity. What does all this prove but that God gives us not merely means sufficient to love Him and be saved, but that it is a rich, overflowing sufficiency, such as one might look for from such boundless Goodness as His.

FRANCIS DE SALES

Our Lord opened my spiritual eye, and showed me my soul in the center of my heart. I saw that my soul was as large as a kingdom, and based on what I saw there, I thought it was a worshipful city. In the center of this city sits our Lord Jesus, true God and true man.

JULIAN OF NORWICH

You want me to tell you why and in what measure God is to be loved. I reply, the reason for loving God is God himself, and the measure, is to love without measure.

BERNARD OF CLAIRVAUX

The prayer of quiet, then, is a little spark of the true love of Himself, which our Lord begins to enkindle in the soul; and His will is, that the soul should understand what this love is by the joy it brings.

TERESA OF ÁVILA

It is impossible to make progress otherwise than by doing and suffering everything in silence.

JOHN OF THE CROSS

We must focus all our attention on the meek stirring of love in our will. As for all other sweetnesses and consolations, sensible or spiritual, no matter how pleasing they are, no matter how holy, we should simply take no heed.

ANONYMOUS (*THE CLOUD OF UNKNOWING*)

Isaiah saw the Lord with His train filling the temple, felt his lips cleansed, and heard the call "who will go?" Ezekiel saw the indescribable living creature with the hands of a man under the wings of the Spirit and heard himself called to his feet for his commission. So here, there was a sudden invading consciousness from beyond. The world with its solid hills appears only the fragment, which it is, and the World of wider Reality floods in and reveals itself. The sky seems rent apart, the Spirit, as though once more brooding over a world in the making, covers Him from above, and gives inward birth to a conviction of uniqueness of Life and uniqueness of mission. He feels Himself in union with His Father.

This experience of the invading Life, awakening a consciousness of unique personal mission, brought with it, as an unavoidable sequence, the stress and strain of a very real temptation. The inner world of self-consciousness has strange watershed "divides" that shape the currents of the life as the mountain ridges of the outer world do the rivers. No new nativity, no fresh awakening, can come to a soul without forcing the momentous issue of its further meaning, or without raising the urgent question, how shall the new insight, the fresh light, the increased power be wrought into life?

RUFUS JONES

Whenever our human understanding grows dark,
With the lament in our heart we awaken divine love.

MECHTHILD OF MAGDEBURG

Ask for an interior knowledge of Our Lord, who became human
for me, that I may love him more intensely and follow him more
closely.

IGNATIUS OF LOYOLA

VI.

Mystics start small. The "bigger, better, faster, louder" ethos of our secular society offers nothing to the person who finds delight and grounding in the heart of Love. Again and again, those who most fully embrace the mystery of God realize that, in light of the Divine, all other goods, or honors, or benchmarks for "success" or "self-esteem" simply fade away into irrelevance. Far from obsessing over earthly standards of greatness or pride, God delights in simplicity, earthiness, lowliness, and calm self-forgetfulness. Humility is not humiliation (which, too often, is simply pride turned inside out), but rather gently remembering "it's not about me." To be contemplative, be humble.

Lead a life worthy of the calling to which you have been called, with all humility and gentleness, with patience, bearing with one another in love, making every effort to maintain the unity of the Spirit in the bond of peace.

EPHESIANS 4:1-3

It is only through the mood of humble and loving receptivity in which the artist perceives beauty, that the human spirit can apprehend a reality which is greater than itself. The many declarations about noughting, poverty, and "holy nothingness" refer to this. The meek and poor of spirit really are the inheritors of Eternity.

EVELYN UNDERHILL

The Little Book of Christian Mysticism

Humility causes us to avoid troubling ourselves about our own imperfections by remembering those of others: for why should we be more perfect than others?—and in the same way to avoid troubling ourselves over those of others when we remember our own: for why should we think it extraordinary for others to have imperfections since we have plenty? Humility makes our hearts gentle towards the perfect and the imperfect; towards those from reverence, towards these from compassion.

Francis de Sales

God loves us endlessly, and we sin customarily, and he shows us our sin gently and mildly. And then we sorrow and mourn discretely, but then we turn to the beholding of his mercy, holding on to his love and goodness, seeing that he is our medicine, since we do nothing but sin. And so by the meekness that comes from the sight of our sin, from faithfully knowing his everlasting love, and from thanking and praising him, we please him.

Julian of Norwich

These are the three steps of truth. We ascend the first by striving to be humble, the second by compassion, the third in the ecstasy of contemplation. In the first, Truth is discovered to be severe; in the second, holy; in the third, pure. Reason leads to the first, in which we think about ourselves. Affection leads to the second, in which we think about others. Purity leads to the third, in which we are lifted up to see what is out of sight.

BERNARD OF CLAIRVAUX

Learn to suffer a little for the love of God without telling everyone about it.

TERESA OF ÁVILA

Ignorance does not know what wisdom is. They who consider themselves gifted with knowledge are, in the eyes of God, most ignorant—"professing themselves to be wise, they become fools." (Romans 1:22)

JOHN OF THE CROSS

Humility is nothing but truly knowing and feeling yourself, as you truly are.

ANONYMOUS (*THE CLOUD OF UNKNOWING*)

Until the heart has become humble, it will not rest from distraction. Humility restrains the heart. And as soon as you have become humble, mercy will surround and envelop you.

ISAAC THE SYRIAN

It is impossible to say too often or too strongly that human nature, body and soul together, is the material for God's will in us . . . it is really through ordinary human life and the things of every hour of every day that union with God comes about.

CARYLL HOUSELANDER

I think the answer to our problems is to confess our faults and to humble ourselves before God. I advise you against long discourses during mental prayer, for they often foster distractions. Remain before God like a poor, mute paralytic at the door of a rich man. Strive to be attentive to God's presence. If your mind wanders or withdraws occasionally, don't get upset. Since these disturbances tend to distract the mind rather than focus it, we must use the will to gently collect our thoughts. If you persevere in this manner God will have mercy on you.

BROTHER LAWRENCE OF THE RESURRECTION

VII.

God loves us. It's a central truth of the Christian faith. And it's not a conditional love, a love based on performance or as a reward for particular behavior. God loves us, no matter what—lavishly, joyfully, infinitely, delightfully. For mystics, this is not an abstract, theoretical love: it is as real as the solid earth and the luminous sunlight. To be a mystic, therefore, means to burn with a desire to respond with purpose and commitment to the singular demands of that love. For while God's love is unconditional, its very purity calls for nothing less than a complete and all-generous response. Such response begins with radical mindfulness, where we listen to God's call. Then we act—which is the heart of obedience.

If you love me, you will keep my commandments… I am in my Father, and you in me, and I in you… Peace I leave with you; my peace I give to you. I do not give to you as the world gives. Do not let your hearts be troubled, and do not let them be afraid.

JESUS (JOHN 14:15, 20, 27)

Contemplation is, on the one hand, the essential activity of all artists; on the other, the art through which those who choose to learn and practice it may share in some fragmentary degree, according to their measure, the special experience of the mystic and the poet. By it they may achieve that virginal outlook upon things, that celestial power of communion with veritable life, which comes when that which we call "sensation" is freed from the tyranny of that which we call "thought."

EVELYN UNDERHILL

Keep, I pray you, your heart exalted very high; attach it indissolubly to the will of that most merciful and fatherly heart of our God. Let it forever be obeyed, and supremely obeyed, by our souls. So long as God wills that we are to be in the world for the love of himself, remain there willing and cheerfully.

FRANCIS DE SALES

We shall all be endlessly gathered in God, truly seeing and fully feeling, and hearing God spiritually and delectably smelling him and sweetly swallowing him.

JULIAN OF NORWICH

Would you know if you belong to His people, or, rather, do you wish to be one of His disciples? Do what Jesus commands, and He will number you among His followers.

BERNARD OF CLAIRVAUX

Look upon yourself as the servant of all: see Christ in others and you will show them respect and reverence.

TERESA OF ÁVILA

The [mystical] way of life demands little trouble and care, it demands denial of the will rather than much knowledge; he who inclines to pleasure and sweetness will be the less able to travel on it.

JOHN OF THE CROSS

If you do not wish to err, see to it that you do not judge others— seek only to listen and to understand. If God calls you, give praise to God, and pray that you do not fall. If God does not seem to call you, pray humbly that God may call you, according to God's will.

ANONYMOUS (*THE BOOK OF PRIVY COUNSELING*)

Devote yourself often to prayer.

BENEDICT OF NURSIA

The Little Book of Christian Mysticism

Truly it is a trustworthy word and deserving of every welcome, your almighty Word, Lord, which in such deep silence made its way down from the Father's royal throne and speaks to us better by its silence. Hear what this loving and mysterious silence of the eternal Word speaks to us. He speaks peace for the holy people upon whom reverence for him and his example impose a religious silence.

GUERRIC OF IGNY

May God grant us all the grace of inner stillness, and thereby the birth of His Divine Word in our souls.

JOHN TAULER

First, then, a man loves his own self for self's sake . . . but when he sees that he is not able to subsist by himself, that God is necessary to him, he begins to inquire and to love God by faith. Thus he loves God in the second place, but because of his own interest, and not for the sake of God Himself. But when, on account of his own necessity, he has begun to worship Him and to approach Him by meditation, by reading, by prayer, by obedience, he comes little by little to know God with a certain familiarity, and in consequence to find Him sweet and kind; and thus having tasted how sweet the Lord is, he passes to the third stage, and thus loves God no longer on account of his own interest, but for the sake of God Himself.

BERNARD OF CLAIRVAUX

The Little Book of Christian Mysticism

VIII.

Historically, one word often associated with the spiritual life—particularly as found in monasteries or convents—is *obedience*. It is a word that has fallen out of favor in our day, since it is often associated with submission and might even imply, to many people's minds, an almost inevitable corruption—as if anyone who would expect the spiritual obedience of another would therefore be unworthy to receive it.

But it's a mistake to limit our understanding of spiritual obedience in terms of earthly power. True obedience, ultimately, belongs to God alone, even if we may express our obedience to God by obeying an earthly master.

Perhaps what is best to remember is that the Latin root for *obedience* does not mean submission so much as deep *listening*. We most fully obey God by mindfully listening for God's direction in our lives.

If the spirituality of obedience begins with listening, it culminates in radical trust. To trust God means to intentionally relinquish control—and in so doing, it creates the space to receive miracles. We have to get out of our own way.

Trust in the Lord with all your heart,
and do not rely on your own insight.
In all your ways acknowledge him,
and he will make straight your paths.

PROVERBS 3:5-6

Faith beholds that which is: Charity loves that which is: Hope alone beholds and loves that which shall be. Faith is static; hope dynamic. Faith is a great tree; hope is the rising sap, the little, swelling bud upon the spray.

EVELYN UNDERHILL

You see, then, that the more we feel ourselves miserable, the more we have occasion to put our trust in God, since we have nothing to rest upon, to enable us to put our trust in ourselves.

FRANCIS DE SALES

Our Lord God is the ground of our beseeching. In God we see two properties: one is authentic prayer, and the other is secure trust. God wills us to be generous in both alike.

JULIAN OF NORWICH

Growth in grace brings expansion of confidence. You will love with greater ardor, and knock on the door with greater assurance, in order to gain what you perceive to be still wanting in you. "The one who knocks will always have the door opened to him."

BERNARD OF CLAIRVAUX

Trust more in the mercy of God and less in your own judgment.

TERESA OF ÁVILA

Love begets a likeness between the lover and the beloved.

JOHN OF THE CROSS

The Little Book of Christian Mysticism

Trust steadfastly, that whatsoever comes, comes to help turn you from impermanent things to God. Without any doing of yours, God will send you one of two things: either an abundance of what is necessary, or the strength and patience to bear being in need.

ANONYMOUS (THE CLOUD OF UNKNOWING)

The will of God is at each moment before us like an immense, inexhaustible ocean that no human heart can fathom; but none can receive from it more than he has the capacity to contain. It is necessary to enlarge this capacity by faith, confidence, and love.

JEAN-PIERRE DE CAUSSADE

Everything is possible for one who believes, still more for one who hopes, even more for one who loves, and most of all for one who practices and perseveres in these three virtues.

BROTHER LAWRENCE OF THE RESURRECTION

Is it, after all, realistic to cling arbitrarily to a single set standard in such a thing as mysticism, in which the great rule is that there are no rules?

THOMAS MERTON

The Little Book of Christian Mysticism

IX.

Repent! It's a religious word that has been badly misused. Street corner preachers, megaphone in hand, screaming at the passersby who largely ignore him, haranguing them to repent—this is what the word has come to mean in our popular mind. But such repentance seems to be more about contrition (feeling sorry for one's sins) than "the new mind" that *metanoia* (the Greek word for repentance) evokes. *Metanoia*—literally "beyond the intellect"—invites us into a new or higher consciousness: the mind of Christ. A mundane way of thinking of it would be as "changing one's mind," which is perhaps what religious repentance ought to mean; but to a mystic, *metanoia* goes far beyond merely rejecting old unhealthy patterns of thinking or behavior. In the silence that is, indeed, "beyond thought," we are invited to remember that we are one with God. In that luminous oneness, destructive or sinful behavior becomes unthinkable.

Let the same mind be in you that was in Christ Jesus,
who, though he was in the form of God,
did not regard equality with God
as something to be exploited,
but emptied himself,
taking the form of a slave,
being born in human likeness.
And being found in human form,
he humbled himself
and became obedient to the point of death—
even death on a cross.

PHILIPPIANS 2:5-8

The first thing that the self observes, when it turns back upon itself in that awful moment of lucidity—enters, as St. Catherine says, into "the cell of self-knowledge,"—is the horrible contrast between its clouded contours and the pure sharp radiance of the Real; between its muddled faulty life, its perverse self-centred drifting, and the clear onward sweep of that Becoming in which it is immersed. It is then that the outlook of rapture and awe receives the countersign of repentance. The harbinger of that new self which must be born appears under the aspect of a desire: a passionate longing to escape from the suddenly perceived hatefulness of selfhood, and to conform to Reality, the Perfect which it has seen under its aspect of Goodness, of Beauty, or of Love—to be worthy of it, in fact to be real.

EVELYN UNDERHILL

Amid the tribulation and mourning of a hearty repentance God often hides the sacred fire of His Love in our heart; and that love first turns to the water of tears, and that again to a glowing fire. Thus it was that the penitent Magdalene loved her Lord, her love turning to tears, and her tears to so great ardour, that, as He said, her sins were forgiven, because "she loved much."

FRANCIS DE SALES

God permits us to fall, and in his blessed love, his might and his wisdom, we are kept. By mercy and grace we are raised to manifold more joys. Thus in righteousness and in mercy, God wills us to know and love him, now and without end. The soul that wisely beholds God in grace receives both abundantly, enjoying him endlessly.

JULIAN OF NORWICH

Charity alone is able to turn the soul away from love of self and of the world to pure love of God. Neither fear nor self-interest can convert the soul. They may change the appearance, perhaps even the conduct, but never the object of supreme desire.

BERNARD OF CLAIRVAUX

We should resolutely give God our heart for His own and should empty it of everything else, that He may take out or put in whatever He pleases as if it were His own property.

TERESA OF ÁVILA

The soul, after it has been definitely converted to the service of God, is, as a rule, spiritually nurtured and caressed by God, even as is the tender child by its loving mother, who warms it with the heat of her bosom and nurtures it with sweet milk and soft and pleasant food, and carries it and caresses it in her arms.

JOHN OF THE CROSS

In the practice of contemplation, God is with us, principally steering and working in us; we merely consent and allow God's action in us, to our great perfection and the spiritual union of our soul with God, in perfect love.

ANONYMOUS (*THE BOOK OF PRIVY COUNSELING*)

As a handful of sand thrown into the great sea, so are the sins of all flesh in comparison with the mind of God. And just as a strongly flowing spring is not obstructed by a handful of dust, so the mercy of the Creator is not stemmed by the vices of His creatures.

ISAAC THE SYRIAN

Faith: the beginning of love.
The end of love: knowledge of God.

EVAGRIUS PONTICUS

It is the modern custom to talk much about the ethics of Jesus and to see in the Sermon on the Mount an ideal of human personality and a program for an ideal social order. But a careful reader cannot fail to feel in Christ's teaching the complete fusion of His ideal for the individual and for society with His consciousness of the world of unseen realities. The new person and the new society are possible in His thought, only through unbroken correspondence with the world of higher forces and of perfect conditions. The only way to be perfect is to be on the way toward likeness to the heavenly Father, the only moral dynamic that will work is a love, like that of God's love, which expels all selfishness and all tendency to stop at partial and inadequate goods.

RUFUS JONES

X.

When dishes are dirty, wash them. When clothes are soiled, launder them. When the soul is stained with the grime of unloving selfishness, mystics present themselves to the Holy Spirit for a deep, purifying cleanse. Like all cleaning tasks, the process of purification that a mystic undergoes is not a one-time chore: alas, it's an ongoing process. To be human means to be continually picking up the grease and grime that comes from ordinary living (let alone from our sinful, selfish, and unloving actions). Of course, we can be like pigs, and simply wallow in our filth—but just as dirty dishes and laundry do not magically disappear, so too the stain of sin never leaves (not even forgiven sin: God loves us enough to set us free from our sins, but also loves us enough to expect us to clean up after ourselves, whether on a physical or spiritual level). But when, with God's help (always with God's help), we embrace the task of scouring away our sins and imperfections, what splendor awaits us—for after all, beneath the grime of a sin-stained soul, something precious awaits our discovery: the image and likeness of God.

Do not be conformed to this world, but be transformed by the renewing of your minds, so that you may discern what is the will of God—what is good and acceptable and perfect.

ROMANS 12:2

What must be the first step of the self upon this road to perfect union with the Absolute? Clearly, a getting rid of all those elements of normal experience which are not in harmony with reality: of illusion, evil, imperfection of every kind. By false desires and false thoughts man has built up for himself a false universe: as a mollusk, by the deliberate and persistent absorption of lime and rejection of all else, can build up for itself a hard shell which shuts it from the external world, and only represents in a distorted and unrecognizable form the ocean from which it was obtained. This hard and wholly unnutritious shell, this one-sided secretion of the surface-consciousness, makes as it were a little cave of illusion for each separate soul. A literal and deliberate getting out of the cave must be for every mystic, as it was for Plato's prisoners, the first step in the individual hunt for reality.

EVELYN UNDERHILL

The Little Book of Christian Mysticism

For the heart being the genuine source of our actions, our works will be always such as our heart is. The Divine Spouse inviting the soul: "Put me as a seal upon thy heart, as a seal upon thy arm." (*Canticle of Canticles* 8–6) Yes, truly; for whosoever has Jesus Christ in his heart will quickly show Him in all his exterior actions.

Francis de Sales

I saw how Christ has compassion on us because of our sin . . . For he says, "I shall break you from your vain affections and your vicious pride; and after that I shall altogether gather you, and make you meek and mild, clean and holy, through union with me."

Julian of Norwich

However, as we are in fleshly bodies, and are born of the desire of the flesh, it is of necessity that our desire, or affection, should begin from the flesh; but if it is rightly directed, advancing step by step under the guidance of grace, it will at length be perfected by the Spirit, because that is not first which is spiritual, but that which is natural, and afterwards that which is spiritual; and it is needful that we should first bear the image of the earthly and afterwards that of the heavenly.

BERNARD OF CLAIRVAUX

Perfect contemplation and divine union are high and supernatural graces given by God to the soul that it may be washed and left stainless and purified from the mire contracted by its sins.

TERESA OF ÁVILA

The soul, when it shall have driven away from itself all that is contrary to the divine will, becomes transformed in God by love.

JOHN OF THE CROSS

Contemplatives desire nothing in particular, but only to behold God. You, likewise, must do the same, as far as grace will allow. Choose God alone, and only God, so that neither your mind nor your will seek anything other than God.

ANONYMOUS (*THE CLOUD OF UNKNOWING*)

Pure love is exercised immediately to God only in pure prayer, by which alone the spirit is united to Him, hence prayer is the only efficacious instrument to obtain supernatural light.

AUGUSTINE BAKER

Just as a covered object left out in the sun cannot be penetrated by the sun's rays, in the same way, once the covering of the soul is removed, the soul opens itself fully to the rays of the sun. The more rust of sin is consumed by fire, the more the soul responds to that love, and its joy increases.

CATHERINE OF GENOA

As the weeping of the time of sowing is followed by the joys of harvest, so are the labors for the sake of God followed by joy.

ISAAC THE SYRIAN

The Little Book of Christian Mysticism

XI.

The light of God's love reveals the shadows of our resistance to that love. Like the penumbra that appear beneath the brilliant sunlight at noon on a summer day, the shadows cast by this shimmering love are dark indeed. Not that this is love's fault! Indeed, sometimes the darkness we encounter is not even the result of sin or evil, but rather simply how our senses fail before the boundlessness of eternity. The heavenly splendor dazzles us so quickly and so thoroughly that the light of God's tender love and mercy appears profoundly dark to us. Yet this is a darkness that illuminates us, even as it blinds us more surely than the most intense light. In that darkness, we are called to surrender all.

While I kept silence, my body wasted away
through my groaning all day long.
For day and night your hand was heavy upon me;
my strength was dried up as by the heat of summer.
Then I acknowledged my sin to you,
and I did not hide my iniquity;
I said, "I will confess my transgressions to the Lord,"
and you forgave the guilt of my sin.

PSALM 32:3-5

The Little Book of Christian Mysticism

Since spiritual no less than physical existence, as we know it, is an endless Becoming, it too has no end. In a sense the whole of the mystical experience in this life consists in a series of purifications, whereby the Finite slowly approaches the nature of its Infinite Source: climbing up the cleansing mountain pool by pool, like the industrious fish in Rulman Merswin's vision, until it reaches its Origin. The greatest of the contemplative saints, far from leaving purgation behind them in their progress, were increasingly aware of their own inadequateness, the nearer they approached to the unitive state: for the true lover of the Absolute, like every other lover, is alternately abased and exalted by his unworthiness and his good fortune. There are moments of high rapture when he knows only that the banner over him is Love: but there are others in which he remains bitterly conscious that in spite of his uttermost surrender there is within him an ineradicable residuum of selfhood, which "stains the white radiance of eternity."

EVELYN UNDERHILL

The kindly forbearance towards another, the trifling victory over temper and passion, the self-denial in some little matter, the resistance to a dislike, the honest acknowledgment of a fault, the effort to be calm and even-tempered, the willingly accepted humiliation and censure,—all these things, be sure, are a more precious harvest than we are wont to think, provided they be wrought for the love of God.

FRANCIS DE SALES

Our sensuality is grounded in nature, in mercy, and in grace, allowing us to receive gifts that lead us to endless life. For I saw full securely that our substance is in God. And also I saw that in our sensuality, God is.

JULIAN OF NORWICH

What could result from the contemplation of compassion so marvelous and so undeserved, favor so free and so well attested, kindness so unexpected, clemency so unconquerable, grace so amazing, except that the soul should withdraw from all sinful affections, reject all that is inconsistent with God's love, and yield herself wholly to heavenly things? It is no wonder that the Bride, moved by the perfume of these unctions, runs swiftly, all on fire with love, yet reckons herself as loving all too little in return for the Bridegroom's love.

BERNARD OF CLAIRVAUX

We are not angels, for we have a body; to seek to make ourselves angels while we are on the earth, and so much on the earth as I was, is an act of folly. In general, our thoughts must have something to rest on, though the soul may go forth out of itself now and then, or it may be very often so full of God as to be in need of no created thing by the help of which it may recollect itself.

TERESA OF ÁVILA

Souls enter the "dark night" [of the senses] when God draws them out of the state of beginners—that is to say, the state of those who practice spiritual meditation—and leads them into the state of proficients, or contemplatives, which is a stage on the way toward spiritual perfection, which is to say, divine union with God.

JOHN OF THE CROSS

When we sleep, normal bodily functions cease, so that the body may take its full rest, to be nourished and strengthened as the body needs. Likewise, the spiritual sleep (of contemplation), our distracted mind and playful imagination is disciplined and silenced, so that our blessed soul may rest softly in the beholding of God, just as God is, and so find spiritual nourishing and strengthening.

ANONYMOUS (*THE BOOK OF PRIVY COUNSELING*)

Quiet senses give birth to peace in the soul, because they do not allow it to experience strife.

ISAAC THE SYRIAN

The divine will is a deep abyss of which the present moment is the entrance. If you plunge into this abyss you will find it infinitely more vast than your desires. Do not flatter anyone, nor worship your own illusions. They can neither give you anything nor receive anything from you. Receive your fullness from the will of God alone, it will not leave you empty.

JEAN-PIERRE DE CAUSSADE

The more we love God the better our love is.

THOMAS AQUINAS

Part Two

ILLUMINATION

XII.

"If the only prayer you say in your life is 'Thank you,' that would be enough." A friend of mine gave me a beautiful print with these words, attributed to Meister Eckhart. I haven't been able to track down the original source for this saying, but in a way it doesn't matter. Gratitude really *is* enough—no matter who says so. A grateful spirit transforms us from the inside out. Counting your blessings is more than a remedy for insomnia—it reprograms the mind and heart to embrace a God-perspective on all things. Indeed, gratitude opens us to see all things—even suffering—in the light of God's love and grace. Gratitude reveals God everywhere.

And let the peace of Christ rule in your hearts, to which indeed you were called in the one body. And be thankful.

COLOSSIANS 3:15

Here is our little planet, chiefly occupied, to our view, in rushing round the sun; but perhaps found from another angle to fill quite another part in the cosmic scheme. And on this apparently unimportant speck, wandering among systems of suns, the appearance of life and its slow development and ever-increasing sensitization; the emerging of pain and of pleasure; and presently man with his growing capacity for self-affirmation and self-sacrifice, for rapture and for grief. Love with its unearthly happiness, unmeasured devotion, and limitless pain; all the ecstasy, all the anguish that we extract from the rhythm of life and death. It is much, really, for one little planet to bring to birth. And presently another music, which some—not many perhaps yet, in comparison with its population—are able to hear. The music of a more inward life, a sort of fugue in which the eternal and temporal are mingled; and here and there some, already, who respond to it. Those who hear it would not all agree as to the nature of the melody; but all would agree that it is something different in kind from the rhythm of life and death. And in their surrender to this—to which, as they feel sure, the physical order too is really keeping time—they taste a larger life; more universal, more divine.

EVELYN UNDERHILL

The lively consideration of favors received makes us humble, because a knowledge of them begets gratitude.

FRANCIS DE SALES

God enjoys being our father, and God enjoys being our mother, and God enjoys being our true spouse—our soul is God's beloved. Christ enjoys being our brother, and Jesus enjoys being our savior. These are five high joys, as I understand, in which God wills that we rejoice: praising, thanking, loving, and endlessly blessing God.

JULIAN OF NORWICH

And since the God who loves us, is boundless, eternal, supreme, the greatness of whose love there is no end, and His wisdom is infinite, whose peace passes all understanding—since this is the God who loves us, I say, can we think of repaying him grudgingly?

BERNARD OF CLAIRVAUX

I praise our Lord highly that he is giving you this quiet and the desire to please him in everything, and that he enlightens you at times with such delightful understanding. This is all the work of his great mercy. Well, His Majesty must give the help that matches the trials, and since they are great, so also are the favors.

Teresa of Ávila

Gratitude involves three luminous expressions of love:

1. Thanksgiving for all the blessings and benefits received, whether spiritual or natural;

2. The great delight of praising God through thanksgiving;

3. And the act of thanking God for nothing other than God himself, which is the most delightful form of gratitude.

John of the Cross

I pray and beseech you to behold the course and manner of your calling. Thank God heartily so that, through the help of God's grace, you may stand firm in the manner of spiritual living that you have chosen, withstanding all the subtle attacks of your physical and spiritual enemies, that you may win the crown of life everlasting. Amen.

ANONYMOUS (*THE CLOUD OF UNKNOWING*)

Our knowledge of God is perfected by gratitude: we are thankful and rejoice in the experience of the truth that he is love.

THOMAS MERTON

The soul does everything that it can; it gives thanks and praises to love; it acts and it works for love, it surrenders its whole self for love, and all its works are perfected for love.

But none of this gives the soul any rest, and it is a great torment to long for what it cannot attain.

BEATRICE OF NAZARETH

Rejoice in the Lord. Then certainly religion is not such a thing as it is represented to the world by many men. For it is looked upon as a doleful, troublesome, melancholy thing, hurtful to the body and disquieting to the souls of men. But see whether this is true. Look upon religion in its actions and employment: and what are they? Rejoice and give thanks. Are not these actions grateful and delightful?

BENJAMIN WHICHCOTE

XIII.

"Sin" is one of those religious words that have fallen out of favor in our time. We recognize the importance of taking responsibility for our mistakes and making amends for our wrongs, but we resist the idea that God cares about the mistakes we make (or, worse, that God is offended or angered by them).

Perhaps we need to reframe the way we approach our unloving actions. Rather than seeing them in a legal way (as crimes committed), perhaps we should approach them as symptoms—as an illness that needs curing by the Divine Physician, rather than an offense that demands punishment from an angry God. Either way, the point is the same: since on our own we make harmful choices that cause consequences, the spiritual life calls us to radically reorient not only our behavior, but our inclination and even our very minds (recognizing that such a radical reorientation can only happen through Divine mercy and grace).

God is the healer, sin is the sickness, we are the patients. The mystical life is the therapy and the cure. But mysticism is more than just a treatment: it invites us to wellness beyond our imagining.

Rejoice with Jerusalem, and be glad for her,
all you who love her;
rejoice with her in joy,
all you who mourn over her—
that you may nurse and be satisfied
from her consoling breast;
that you may drink deeply with delight
from her glorious bosom.
For thus says the Lord . . .
As a mother comforts her child,
so I will comfort you;
you shall be comforted in Jerusalem.

ISAIAH 66:10-13

Human life is readjusted and made whole by the healing action of dynamic love, exercised by One whose life is identical with His prayer. His injunctions to His agents follow the same lines. They are to heal disharmony and misery wherever they find it; meeting with an eager and compassionate love the most repulsive aspects of life, touching the leper, ministering to the neurotic, seeking the degraded and the lost.

EVELYN UNDERHILL

For whether the Holy Spirit strengthens us by His inspirations or by the love He sheds within the heart; whether His succor raises and bears us, or gives us strength to go of ourselves, come what may, it is through Him that we live and move and have our being.

FRANCIS DE SALES

For this is the great deed that our Lord God shall do . . . he shall make well all that is not well.

JULIAN OF NORWICH

To be attentive to God's presence is to listen, to pray, to lift up our hearts to God, and to lay aside our ever-present inner chatter. Lectio divina is the tool of choice to fill our hearts and minds with the Word of God rather than with our inner words and interpersonal traumas. To do this, we might memorize some of the psalms, for instance, or know one of the gospels in its entirety. We commit ourselves to follow the example of Christ's teaching, his healing, and his love for all. Our reference becomes Christ, the Holy Spirit instructing and filling us with an impulse to love.

MARY MARGARET FUNK

The principal object of one who begins to make use of prayer (do not forget this, for it is important), should be to endeavor and resolve, and dispose oneself, with all possible diligence, to conform his will to that of God: be assured, as I shall afterwards mention, that herein consists all that high perfection which we should attain in our spiritual progress.

TERESA OF ÁVILA

This Obscure Night is a certain inflowing of God into the soul, which cleanses it of its ignorances and imperfections, habitual, natural, and spiritual. Contemplatives call it infused contemplation, or Mystical Theology, whereby God secretly teaches the soul and instructs it in the perfection of love, without efforts on its own part beyond loving attention to God, listening to His voice and admitting the light He sends, without understanding how this is infused contemplation. It is the loving Wisdom of God that produces special effects in the soul, for it prepares it, by enlightening it for union with God in love: that loving Wisdom, which by enlightening purifies the blessed spirits, is that which here purifies and enlightens the soul.

JOHN OF THE CROSS

For the love of God, govern yourself discreetly both in body and soul, and keep as healthy as you can. But when you do fall sick, patiently and humbly wait for God's mercy, and all is then good enough.

ANONYMOUS (*THE CLOUD OF UNKNOWING*)

At times it may feel as though nothing is happening in that vast silence. And yet *so much is happening!* In the endless region of our inner landscape, bit by tiny bit, we are transformed into the likeness of Christ, as we are changed by waves and waves of Silent Mercy; so that gradually we come to speak, think, and love as Christ does: gently, without fuss, in a marvel of beauty.

ELIAS MARECHAL

It seems to me that I have found my Heaven on earth, since Heaven is God, and God is [in] my soul. The day I understood that, everything became clear to me. I would like to whisper this secret to those I love so they too might always cling to God through everything.

ELIZABETH OF THE TRINITY

For each has within him a secret of the Divinity; each is growing towards the revelation of that secret to himself, and so to the full reception, according to his measure, of the divine.

GEORGE MACDONALD

XIV.

In the mystical life, memory is more than just an imprint from the past: it is a doorway into awareness which transcends time. Contemplation invites us to remember more than just what happened a long time ago—it invites us to "remember" the real and deep presence of God in our lives, a presence that we often forget beneath the frenzy and freneticism of our overly busy lives. One reason why silence matters so much to contemplatives is that it clears a space within our minds and hearts for this kind of sacred remembering to emerge, unhurried and by its own rhythm.

Recollection, in a mystical sense, points to this kind of sacred memory. In recollection, our memory gazes not backward in time, but deeply into the present, into that place where God's presence normally rests hidden from our awareness. The prayer of recollection arises where past, present, and future pour into God's eternal now.

The Lord is in his holy temple;
let all the earth keep silence before him!

HABAKKUK 2:20

Recollection . . . is in essence no more and no less than the subjection of the attention to the control of the will. It is not, therefore, a purely mystical activity. In one form or another it is demanded of all who would get control of their own mental processes; and does or should represent the first great step in the education of the human consciousness. So slothful, however, is man in all that concerns his higher faculties, that few deliberately undertake this education at all. They are content to make their contacts with things by a vague, unregulated power, ever apt to play truant, ever apt to fail them. Unless they be spurred to it by that passion for ultimate things which expresses itself in religion, philosophy, or art, they seldom learn the secret of a voluntary concentration of the mind.

EVELYN UNDERHILL

Prayer places our mind in the brightness and light of God, and exposes our will to the heat of heavenly love. There is nothing that so effectually frees our understanding from its ignorance, or our will from its depraved affections, as prayer. It is the water of benediction which causes the plants of our good desires to grow green and flourish. It cleanses our souls from their imperfections, and quenches the thirst of passion in our hearts.

FRANCIS DE SALES

Prayer rightfully understands that fullness of joy to come, with true longing and secure trust. We naturally long for the bliss to which we are ordained, but which we fail to possess; and we savor in our sweet mind true understanding and love, which graciously makes us trust.

JULIAN OF NORWICH

The Little Book of Christian Mysticism

It is indeed right that those who take no delight in present things should be sustained by the recollection of what is to come, and those who refuse to be consoled by plentiful but mutable things should find joy in thinking of eternity.

BERNARD OF CLAIRVAUX

This is a prayer which brings with it many blessings. It is called recollection because the soul collects together all the faculties and enters within itself to be with its God. Its Divine Master comes more speedily to teach it, and to grant it the Prayer of Quiet, than in any other way.

TERESA OF ÁVILA

Seek by reading and you will find by meditating; cry in prayer and the door will be opened in contemplation.

JOHN OF THE CROSS

For whenever your mind is distracted by any earthly or bodily thing, no matter how good it might be or what good it might lead to, you are still "beneath yourself" in your spiritual practice, and outside the spirit of contemplation.

ANONYMOUS (*THE CLOUD OF UNKNOWING*)

Love and self-mastery free the soul from passions; reading and contemplation deliver the mind from ignorance; and the state of prayer places it with God himself.

MAXIMUS THE CONFESSOR

Be at peace with your own soul, then heaven and earth will be at peace with you. Eagerly enter into the treasure house that is within you, and so you will see the things that are in heaven; for there is but one single entry to them both. The ladder that leads to the Kingdom is hidden within your soul.

ISAAC THE SYRIAN

The Little Book of Christian Mysticism

When we learn how to center down into the stillness and quiet, to listen with our souls for the whisperings of Life and Truth, to bring all our inner powers into parallelism with the set of divine currents, we shall hear tidings from the inner world at the heart and center of which is God.

RUFUS JONES

XV.

When a child plays freely, exuberantly, blissfully, we say she runs with wild abandon. The mystical life calls for a similar abandonment within the splendor of God. To abandon yourself to God is to embrace infinite possibility. It doesn't mean to be passive or to be irresponsible, but rather to commit every aspect of life to the trust that comes from faith. It is a gesture of generosity and willingness—open your life to the continual guidance and leading of the Spirit. There's a joke about the famous twentieth-century dancer Ginger Rogers, who had to do everything her partner Fred Astaire did, only backwards and in heels! Likewise, to abandon yourself to God may seem like you are dancing backwards, wearing shoes that barely touch the floor at all. It can be frightening, but also exhilarating. It all depends on how much we are willing to let go.

"Be still, and know that I am God!"

PSALM 46:10

Moreover, as your meditation becomes deeper it will defend you from the perpetual assaults of the outer world. You will hear the busy hum of that world as a distant exterior melody, and know yourself to be in some sort withdrawn from it. You have set a ring of silence between you and it; and behold! within that silence you are free. You will look at the colored scene, and it will seem to you thin and papery: only one amongst countless possible images of a deeper life as yet beyond your reach. And gradually, you will come to be aware of an entity, a You, who can thus hold at arm's length, be aware of, look at, an idea—a universe—other than itself. By this voluntary painful act of concentration, this first step upon the ladder which goes—as the mystics would say—from "multiplicity to unity," you have to some extent withdrawn yourself from that union with unrealities, with notions and concepts, which has hitherto contented you; and at once all the values of existence are changed. "The road to a Yea lies through a Nay." You, in this preliminary movement of recollection, are saying your first deliberate No to the claim which the world of appearance makes to a total possession of your consciousness: and are thus making possible some contact between that consciousness and the World of Reality.

EVELYN UNDERHILL

Let us now pass on to the other question, which is as to self-abandonment, and what ought to be the exercises of the self-abandoned soul. You must know that to practice self-abandonment and to forsake ourselves, is nothing else but to yield up and get rid of our own will that we may give it to God. For, as I have already said, it would be of no benefit at all to renounce and forsake ourselves, if it were not done in order to unite ourselves perfectly to the divine Goodness.

FRANCIS DE SALES

All shall be well, and all shall be well, and all manner of things shall be well.

JULIAN OF NORWICH

O you, whoever you are, who feel that in the tidal wave of this world you are nearer to being tossed about among the squalls and gales than treading on dry land, if you do not want to founder in the tempest, do not avert your eyes from the brightness of this star. When the wind of temptation blows up within you, when you strike the rock of tribulation, gaze up at this star, call out to Mary. Whether you are being tossed about by the waves of pride or ambition or slander or jealousy, gaze up at this star, call out to Mary.

BERNARD OF CLAIRVAUX

Detach your heart from all things; seek God, and you will find Him.

TERESA OF ÁVILA

The steps on a staircase are merely means to reach the goal, which is the room at the top. If, in climbing them, we do not leave each step behind, or we stop to rest, we will never reach the peaceful summit. Everyone who longs for union with the Supreme Good and Repose must go beyond all the steps of spiritual concepts, images and ideas—for they are not the goal, they merely lead us to the goal—God.

JOHN OF THE CROSS

To speedily attain your spiritual purpose, no other means is necessary than consciousness of God alone, approached with reverence and a stirring of lasting love. Only through God may you attain God. Attend carefully to your stirring of love, and do not scatter your spiritual beholding with distractions—then you may, by grace, find God in your heart.

ANONYMOUS (THE EPISTLE OF DISCRETION)

The essence of spirituality is contained in this phrase: "complete and utter abandonment to the will of God." By that I mean we should never think of ourselves, but be continually occupied with loving and obeying him. We must put aside all those fears, those uneasy broodings, those qualms of conscience, and those anxieties which can arise from the concern we have for achieving holiness and our salvation. As God wants to look after all our affairs, let us leave them all to him so that we can concentrate our whole attention on him.

JEAN-PIERRE DE CAUSSADE

Everything is emptiness and everything is compassion.

THOMAS MERTON

If my eye is to receive an image, it must be free from all other images; for if it already has so much as one, it cannot see another, nor can the ear hear a sound if it be occupied with one already. Any power of receiving must first be empty before it can receive anything.

JOHN TAULER

XVI.

"I am the light of the world," declared Jesus (John 8:12), but he also said, "*You* are the light of the world" (Matthew 5:14). A paradox? Or, perhaps, insight into the essential unity between Christ and creation that forms the foundation of the mystical life?

The light that shines in us is the light of Christ shining through us. This is not something we have to make happen; it is something we must allow to happen. Not something we achieve, something we receive.

Yet to bask in that Christ-light within, we need to open ourselves to receive it.

The sunflower turns over the course of the day so that its blossom always faces the sun. Likewise, mystics continually recalibrate their lives to embrace the Divine light. Illumination may come from within, but its source is heavenly.

The light of the body is the eye: if therefore your eye sees singly (nondually), your whole body will shine like the sun.
But if your eye sees dualistically (looking for evil to judge), your whole body shall be full of darkness.

JESUS (LUKE 11:34)[3]

Illumination shall be gradual. The attainment of it depends not so much upon a philosophy accepted, or a new gift of vision suddenly received, as upon an uninterrupted changing and widening of character; a progressive growth towards the Real, an ever more profound harmonization of the self's life with the greater and inclusive rhythms of existence. It shall therefore develop in width and depth as the sphere of that self's intuitive love extends.

EVELYN UNDERHILL

God wills that we know this: he keeps us ever secure, in woe and in wellness. To profit the soul, God may sometimes seem to leave it, even though the person has not sinned. For sometimes I experienced a sudden sense of being abandoned (even though I hadn't sinned), but then at other times a blissful feeling that I did not deserve. For our Lord gives joy freely when he wills, and other times permits us to suffer, but both arise out of the same love.

JULIAN OF NORWICH

If, then, when the stain of sin and the rust of vice have been burned off in this fire, and your conscience lies unclouded and serene, you experience a sudden unusual expansion of the mind and an impression of light flooding the intellect and giving you a new understanding either of the Scriptures or of the mysteries . . . this, without any doubt, is the eye of the Bridegroom looking on you, and then, as Isaiah says, your light shall rise like the sun and your darkest hour be as the noonday. Not through open doors, but through narrow fissures only—at least while the decrepit wall of our body stands—shall this ray of dazzling light pour itself into our souls.

BERNARD OF CLAIRVAUX

The soul resembles a window; the divine light of the presence of God in the order of nature, perpetually strikes upon it, or rather dwells within it. The soul then by resigning itself— in removing from itself every spot and stain . . . becomes immediately enlightened by, and transformed in, God; because He communicates His own supernatural Being in such a way that the soul seems to be God Himself and to possess the things of God.

JOHN OF THE CROSS

Wherever there is mere light without a will to love, we may fear that there is more of that which "puffs up than that which edifies."

FRANCIS DE SALES

What seems to be living in light when we live on the surface of our being is really to live in darkness. When we withdraw from noise and our own control over our lives and enter into a waiting silence before God to speak His Word we truly make a transition for darkness to light.

GEORGE A. MALONEY, SJ

Wherever God is, there is Heaven. No doubt you can believe that, in any place where His Majesty is, there is fullness of glory.

TERESA OF ÁVILA

A distinct actual supernatural light and grace is necessary; and this not to teach us new precepts or furnish us with new counsels ... For want of which light it is that the true way to perfection is almost unknown, even to those who profess the seeking of perfection, and fill the world with books and instructions about it. By what other means, then, is such light to be had? Surely by no other but by the exercise of divine love, which is most perfectly performed in internal prayer, in attention to and union with God in spirit.

AUGUSTINE BAKER

Sometimes, peradventure, God will send out a beam of spiritual light, piercing the cloud of unknowing that is between you and God, to show you some private revelation, of which mortals may not, or cannot, speak. Then you shall feel your affection inflamed with the fire of God's love, far more than I tell you, or may or will, at this time.

ANONYMOUS (*THE CLOUD OF UNKNOWING*)

When the loving soul gazes into the eternal mirror, she says: "Lord, between you and me all things are beautiful."

MECHTHILD OF MAGDEBURG

XVII.

"Where there is no vision, people perish." Fortunately, mystics are people of vision—indeed, in the popular mind words like "mystic" and "visionary" might almost be synonymous. Writings of mystics like Hildegard of Bingen, Julian of Norwich, and Teresa of Ávila are replete with remarkable stories of vivid, otherworldly visions and voices. Never mind that other mystics take a cautious, if not skeptical, approach to such extraordinary phenomena. There's something about the mystical life that seems to call people out of the ordinary structures of their mind and reality into a place of pure possibility and wonder, where the encounter with God—or the angels or the saints, or even just a sanctified engagement with one's own unconscious—is an invitation into a new mind, a new heart, a new way of seeing.

If we broaden our understanding of "vision" to include something beyond just the supernatural kind, then we have an even more inclusive approach to mystics and the mystical experience. Ultimately, whether supernatural or merely deeply intuitive, the "vision" of the mystics is a vision of hope, of joy, of compassion, of community. To behold God is to behold love.

Then afterward I will pour out my spirit on all flesh; your sons and your daughters shall prophesy, your old men shall dream dreams, and your young men shall see visions. Even on the male and female slaves, in those days, I will pour out my spirit. I will show portents in the heavens and on the earth, blood and fire and columns of smoke. The sun shall be turned to darkness, and the moon to blood, before the great and terrible day of the Lord comes.

JOEL 2:28-31

The real mystical life, which is the truly practical life, begins at the beginning; not with supernatural acts and ecstatic apprehensions, but with the normal faculties of the normal man. "I do not require of you," says Teresa to her pupils in meditation, "to form great and curious considerations in your understanding: I require of you no more than to look."

EVELYN UNDERHILL

God has set His mark on all creation, so that the knowledge we attain of Him in His creatures is truly like a sight of His Footprints; while compared with that, faith is a sight of His Very Face.

FRANCIS DE SALES

I am not good because of my visions, but am good only if I love God better—and if you love God better, than my visions are more for you than for me.

JULIAN OF NORWICH

I admit that the Word has also come to me—I speak as a fool—and has come many times. But although he has come to me, I have never been conscious of the moment of his coming. I perceived his presence, I remembered afterward that he had been with me; sometimes I had a presentiment that he would come, but I was never conscious of his coming or his going.

BERNARD OF CLAIRVAUX

The soul recognizes the presence of God by the effects which, as I say, He produces in the soul, for it is by that means that His Majesty is pleased to make His presence felt: but in a vision the soul distinctly sees that Jesus Christ, the Son of the Virgin, is present.

TERESA OF ÁVILA

The pure in heart find in all things the knowledge of God, sweet, chaste, pure, spiritual, joyous, and loving.

JOHN OF THE CROSS

I pray you: seek more to embody God than to merely have knowledge of God. For knowledge can deceive us with pride, but a meek, loving awareness will not deceive. Knowledge puffs up, but love builds up (I Corinthians 8:1). Knowledge leads to travail, whereas awareness leads to rest.

ANONYMOUS (*THE BOOK OF PRIVY COUNSELING*)

But now see what it is to adore God: it is, in the Christian faith, with great reverence and above reason, to gaze in the spirit upon God, the Eternal Power, Creator and Lord of heaven and earth and all that in them is.

JOHN RUUSBROEC

Spiritual vision is much sharper and far clearer than corporeal vision. It is like the sudden illumination by a bolt of lightning, that in a dark night allows things to stand out clear and distinct for a moment. Under the influence of the spiritual light, the objects seen are impressed so deeply on the soul that every time she adverts to them by the grace of God, she beholds them as she did the first time.

EDITH STEIN

As God can only be seen by His own light, so He can only be loved by His own love.

MEISTER ECKHART

XVIII.

The Pagan philosopher Plotinus described mysticism as "the flight of the alone to the Alone." It's a poetic and evocative image—Evelyn Underhill quotes it repeatedly—but for Christians, it only tells part of the story. Christian spirituality sees in God not only the "Aloneness" of God's oneness, but also the "Community" of the Three Persons of the Holy Trinity. Likewise, spirituality is not just about each creature as an individual, but about how we all together form the Mystical Body of Christ. So for Christian mystics, at least, it makes just as much sense to talk about "the flight of the community to the Trinity."

"If I live alone, whose feet shall I wash?" This question was directed toward the hermits who lived in the deserts of Egypt, Syria, and Palestine; it was a sober reminder that salvation (or, for that matter, mystical union with God) is never a do-it-all-by-yourself deal. It's a question that remains relevant today. We are called into the inner room—but also out again, to serve others.

For where two or three are gathered in my name, I am there among them.

JESUS (MATTHEW 18:20)

The full life of the Spirit, then, is active, contemplative, ascetic and apostolic; though nowadays we express these abiding human dispositions in other and less formidable terms. If we translate them as work, prayer, self-discipline and social service they do not look quite so bad. But even so, what a tremendous program to put before the ordinary human creature, and how difficult it looks when thus arranged! That balance to be discovered and held between due contact with this present living world of time, and due renunciation of it. That continual penetration of the time-world with the spirit of Eternity.

EVELYN UNDERHILL

It certainly is a rare thing, my child, in a large community not to find someone who is a trial, but that so many are good is a great subject of consolation.

JANE FRANCES DE CHANTAL

We are all one in love.

JULIAN OF NORWICH

Either you are one of the foolish virgins . . . or one of the wise. If you are one of the foolish, you need your community; if one of the wise, your community needs you.

BERNARD OF CLAIRVAUX

Be indulgent to others, rigorous to yourself.

TERESA OF ÁVILA

When the love and affection we give to another created being is spiritual and grounded in God, then the love of God grows with it. The more we remember that earthly love, the more we also remember and long for God: one love grows alongside the other.

JOHN OF THE CROSS

Judge yourself all you want, for it is a matter between you and your God (or between you and your spiritual director). But leave others alone.

ANONYMOUS (*THE CLOUD OF UNKNOWING*)

When a life is set on fire, and is radiant with self-consuming love, it will invariably set other lives on fire. Such a person may teach many valuable ideas, he may organize many movements, he may attack many evil customs, but the best thing he will ever do will be to fuse and kindle other souls with the fire of his passion. His own burning, shining life is always his supreme service.

RUFUS JONES

If you want to love the whole Christ you have to open wide your heart; because Christ is the Head of a Body in Heaven, at the right hand of the Father, but he is also present in each member of this same Body . . . in each one of us.

AUGUSTINE OF HIPPO

What can be a greater vision than this: to see the invisible God in a visible person?

PACHOMIUS

XIX.

The Bible says "the fear of the Lord is the beginning of wisdom" (Psalm 111:10). But it's not the *end* of wisdom—a subtle fact that too many Christians overlook. Indeed, fear may be a starting point for some people's spiritual journey (after a near-death experience, for example, or coming to grips with an addiction or some other problem), but a healthy spirituality moves, sooner or later, from fear to love: "There is no fear in love, but perfect love casts out fear . . ." (I John 4:18).

Likewise, the mystical way may begin in longing, but the point behind longing is to seek fulfillment—and for mystics and contemplatives, that path leads to compassion. The longing may never fully leave us (the Bible doesn't promise that "love will cast out desire"!), but it finds at least a partial fulfillment in the encounter with Divine love. The love of God is infinite, vast, transformational, generous. If flows to us, and, if we allow, it flows through us. In that flow is life.

And if I have prophetic powers, and understand all mysteries and all knowledge, and if I have all faith, so as to remove mountains, but do not have love, I am nothing.

I CORINTHIANS 13:2

The spiritual life is not upon the heavenly hearth-rug, within safe distance from the Fire of Love. It demands, indeed, very often things so hard that seen from the hearth-rug they seem to us superhuman: immensely generous compassion, forbearance, forgiveness, gentleness, radiant purity, self-forgetting zeal. It means a complete conquest of life's perennial tendency to lag behind the best possible; willing acceptance of hardship and pain.

EVELYN UNDERHILL

The best prayer is that which keeps us so occupied with God that we don't think about ourselves or about what we are doing.

FRANCIS DE SALES

Our Lord showed me a little thing, the size of a hazelnut, in the palm of my hand; and it was as round as a ball. I looked thereupon with eye of my understanding, and thought: "What may this be?" And I received this answer: "It is all that is made."

I marveled how it might last, for I thought it might suddenly have fallen to nothingness, for how little it was. And I was answered in my understanding: "It lasts, and ever shall, for God loves it." And so all things have their being by the love of God.

In this little thing I saw three properties. The first is that God made it, the second is that God loves it, the third, that God keeps it.

JULIAN OF NORWICH

Whosoever truly loves God also loves all God's creatures. Such love is pure, and finds no burden in the precept bidding us to purify our souls, in obeying the truth through the Spirit with unfeigned love for all people. To love as we ought to love is seen as a just command. Such love is praiseworthy, since it is spontaneous; pure, since it is revealed not in words, but in deeds; just, since it repays what it has received. Everyone who loves like this, loves even as they are loved, and seek no more for themselves but only those things which are Christ's—just as Jesus sought not His own welfare, but ours, or rather ourselves. Such was the love sung by the psalmist: "O give thanks unto the Lord, for God is gracious." Whoever praises God for God's essential goodness, and not merely because of the benefits God bestows on us, really does love God for God's sake, and not for selfish reasons.

BERNARD OF CLAIRVAUX

The important thing is not to think much, but to love much; do, then, whatever most arouses you to love.

TERESA OF ÁVILA

Love unites the soul with God, and the greater its love the deeper does it enter into God, and the more is it centered in Him.

JOHN OF THE CROSS

Charity for your fellow Christians is truly and perfectly fulfilled in contemplative prayer. For the seasoned contemplative has no special regard for any individual, whether a close relative or a stranger, a friend or a foe. To the contemplative, all people are alike, like a kinsman, and no one is a stranger. Contemplatives consider all people as friends, and none as foes.

ANONYMOUS (*THE CLOUD OF UNKNOWING*)

The best masters say that the love wherewith we love is the Holy Spirit. Some deny it. But this is always true: all those motives by which we are moved to love, in these is nothing else than the Holy Spirit.

MEISTER ECKHART

Behold the miracle! Love has no awareness of merit or demerit— it has no scale by which its portion may be weighed or measured. It does not seek to balance giving and receiving. Love loves; that is its nature. But this does not mean that love is blind, naive or pretentious. It does mean that love holds its object securely in its grasp calling all that it sees by its true name but surrounding all with a wisdom born both of its passion and its understanding.

HOWARD THURMAN

The reason for loving one's neighbor is a theological reason which closely relates it to the love of God. They are not two parallel loves, nor is love of neighbor a subordinate love. It is the two sides of one love, as one is the love within the Trinity and one the love with which Christ loves the Father and humankind.

PEDRO ARRUPE

The Little Book of Christian Mysticism

XX.

God comes to us in so many ways. We do not only find God in "spiritual" activities such as prayer and meditation and worship—worthy though such activities may be. But God is not just found in monasteries, or churches, or sacred sites. God is the God of all time and space, so God is literally everywhere—and everywhen.

We do not so much need to search for God, as to be still long enough to allow God to find us.

God comes to us through people, whether loved ones, family, friends, even neighbors and strangers—even, sometimes, in an adversary or an opponent, even an enemy. (Jesus is clear that loving one's enemies is not optional for Christians!) But we may also receive God through nature, through art, through music and poetry, through stories, through daydreams and the imagination, and of course through love. When we reflect on those infinite ways God comes to us, we meditate on the invitation to move deeper into the limitless, loving mystery.

On the glorious splendor of your majesty,
. . . and on your wondrous works, I will meditate.

PSALM 145:5

The Little Book of Christian Mysticism

Now meditation is a half-way house between thinking and contemplating: and as a discipline, it derives its chief value from this transitional character. The real mystical life, which is the truly practical life, begins at the beginning; not with supernatural acts and ecstatic apprehensions, but with the normal faculties of the normal man.

EVELYN UNDERHILL

The summer bee flits from flower to flower, not at haphazard, but designedly; not merely to recreate itself amid the garden's pleasant design, but to seek honey, and carry it to its hive, to the symmetric comb where it stores its winter food. Even so the devout soul in meditation. It goes from mystery to mystery, not merely as dipping into the beauty of those wondrous matters, but deliberately seeking fresh motives for love and devout affections; and having found these, it feeds upon and imbibes them, and, storing them up within, condenses them into resolutions suitable to the time of temptation. Thus the Heavenly Bride of the Canticles hovers like a bee round the cheek, the lips, the locks of her Beloved, drawing thence innumerable delights, until, kindled with sacred joy, she talks with Him, questions, harkens, sighs, longs, marvels, while He fills her with content, opens her heart, and fills it with boundless light and sweetness.

FRANCIS DE SALES

For in faith, with hope and charity, our life is grounded.

JULIAN OF NORWICH

All that is good, everything that is perfect, is given us from above; it comes down from the Father of all light. For this ointment is made from the gifts of God bestowed on the human race. Happy the one who gathers these gifts carefully and keeps them in mind with due thanksgiving. When they shall have been pounded and refined in the heart's receptacle with the pestle of frequent meditation, all of them fused together in the fire of holy desire, and finally enriched with the oil of gladness, you will have an ointment excellent and precious.

BERNARD OF CLAIRVAUX

If you had asked me about meditation, I could have instructed you, and I advise every one to practice it even though they do not possess the virtues, for this is the first step to obtain them all: it is most essential for all Christians to begin this practice.

TERESA OF ÁVILA

The purpose of meditation and reflection on the nature of God is to foster deeper knowledge and love of God. Each time a soul does this, especially when repeated often enough to form a habit, it fosters an ongoing sense of loving knowledge of God within the soul.

JOHN OF THE CROSS

The disobedience of the imagination may clearly be conceived in those who are newly turned from worldly life to the practice of devotion in prayer. For until their imagination be disciplined by the light of grace and reason, through the continual practice of spiritual meditation on topics such as their own brokenness, the passion and kindness of our Lord God, among others—they remain incapable of putting away the wonderful and diverse thoughts, fantasies, and images that distract their consciousness, through the light and the curiosity of the imagination.

ANONYMOUS (*THE CLOUD OF UNKNOWING*)

When all impurity has been purged, these things lift up the eyes of the heart: meditation of the marvelous essence of God, examination of pure truth, clean and strong prayer, joyful praise, and burning desire for God. Embrace these things and live in them and run to meet the life-giving light which is offered to you as God's children (Hebrews 12:7) and is abundantly poured forth in your minds.

ELISABETH OF SCHÖNAU

The poorest, simplest soul living in the world, and following the common life of good Christians there, if she will faithfully correspond to the internal light and tracts afforded her by God's Spirit, may as securely, yea, and sometimes more speedily, arrive to the top of the mountain of vision than the most learned doctors, the most profoundly wise men, yea, the most abstracted confined hermits.

AUGUSTINE BAKER

No one knows what goes on in the depths of our souls. To sense God near, to meditate, to pray, to gather our thoughts so as to reflect on them more deeply, that is to live the inner life, and this interior life is the greatest joy.

ÉLISABETH LESEUR

XXI.

"**R**ejoice always, pray without ceasing, give thanks in all circumstances; for this is the will of God in Christ Jesus for you," wrote Saint Paul to the Thessalonians; he went on to say, "Do not quench the Spirit" (I Thessalonians 5:16-19). It seems that, as we advance on the contemplative path, joy, prayer, gratitude, all flow together, creating something greater than the sum of their parts: a heart opened to the guidance of the Holy Spirit.

Faith requires hope and love, and love requires joy and peace. Each needs the others. Peace invites us deep into silence, whereas joy invites us to embrace an expanded awareness. In joy we see from a new perspective.

I bow my knees before the Father, from whom every family in heaven and on earth takes its name. I pray that, according to the riches of his glory, he may grant that you may be strengthened in your inner being with power through his Spirit, and that Christ may dwell in your hearts through faith, as you are being rooted and grounded in love. I pray that you may have the power to comprehend, with all the saints, what is the breadth and length and height and depth, and to know the love of Christ that surpasses knowledge, so that you may be filled with all the fullness of God.

EPHESIANS 3:14-19

It is to Mechthild of Magdeburg, whose contemplation was emphatically of the intimate type, that we owe the most perfect definition of this communion of the mystic with his Friend. "Orison," she says, "draws the great God down into the small heart: it drives the hungry soul out to the full God. It brings together the two lovers, God and the soul, into a joyful room where they speak much of love."

EVELYN UNDERHILL

Ecstasy is called rapture because by it God draws and raises us to Himself; and rapture is called ecstasy because it carries us forcibly out of ourselves and unites us to God. The attractions whereby God draws us are marvelously sweet; yet at the same time the power with which His Divine Beauty and Goodness act upon the soul is so intense, that it ravishes and carries it away, while the eagerness with which the raptured soul yields to His attractions causes it not merely to rise up, but to rush, so to say, out of itself into the Bosom of its God.

FRANCIS DE SALES

In this blissed revelation I was truly taught that whatever man or woman willfully chooses God in this life, he or she may be secure that he or she is chosen by God. Keep this truly, for so it is God's will that we rest secure, trusting the bliss of heaven while we are still here on earth, as we shall be likewise secure when we go there.

JULIAN OF NORWICH

The faithful soul longs and pants for God, and rests sweetly in the memory of him. Until the glory of his face is revealed, she glories in the reproach of the Cross. Like the Bride, the dove of Christ, covered with silver wings (Psalm 68:13), white with innocence and purity, she reposes in the thought of your abundant kindness, Lord Jesus; and above all she longs for that day when in the joyful splendor of your saints, gleaming with the radiance of the Beatific Vision, her feathers shall be like gold, resplendent with the joy of your countenance.

BERNARD OF CLAIRVAUX

If possible avoid revealing your interior devotion. "My secret is for myself," said St. Francis and St. Bernard.

TERESA OF ÁVILA

They who are already perfect receive these Divine visitations in peace and in the sweetness of love: their ecstasies cease, for they were only graces to prepare them for this more perfect condition.

JOHN OF THE CROSS

"Your vats will be bursting with wine" (Proverbs 3:10) . . . in Holy Scripture, this wine is verily and mystically understood to be spiritual wisdom, in true contemplation and high savor of the Godhead. And all this shall be done suddenly, lustily and graciously, without any travail or effort on your part, only by the ministration of angels through the power of their loving, hidden work.

ANONYMOUS (THE LETTER OF PRIVATE DIRECTION)

The overwhelming love of God gives the soul a joy beyond words.

CATHERINE OF GENOA

O love, to see you is to be in ecstasy in God. To cling to you is to be joined to God by a nuptial contract. O serenest light of my soul, very brightest morning, ah, break into day in me now and begin so to shine for me that by your light I may see light and that through you my night may be turned into day.

GERTRUDE THE GREAT

This embrace of God sets ablaze a fire within the soul with which the whole soul burns for Christ. It also produces a light so great that the soul understands the fullness of God's goodness, which it experiences in itself, and which is, moreover, much greater than the soul's experience of it. The effect then of this fire within the soul is to render it certain and secure that Christ is within it. And yet, what we have said is nothing in comparison to what this experience really is.

ANGELA OF FOLIGNO

XXII.

The mystical life invites us into expanded awareness. We see all things not only from a place beyond ourselves, but even from a place above ourselves. We give ourselves to God, and God expands our minds and our hearts, presumably to make them big enough to carry God's love, God's compassion, God's wisdom, God's mercy. When we give ourselves to God, God teaches us to fly.

I know a person in Christ who fourteen years ago was caught up to the third heaven—whether in the body or out of the body I do not know; God knows. And I know that such a person— whether in the body or out of the body I do not know; God knows—was caught up into Paradise and heard things that are not to be told, that no mortal is permitted to repeat . . . to keep me from being too elated, a thorn was given me in the flesh, a messenger of Satan to torment me, to keep me from being too elated. Three times I appealed to the Lord about this, that it would leave me, but he said to me, "My grace is sufficient for you, for power is made perfect in weakness." So, I will boast all the more gladly of my weaknesses, so that the power of Christ may dwell in me.

THE APOSTLE PAUL (II CORINTHIANS 12:2-4, 7-9)

The Little Book of Christian Mysticism

The condition of joyous and awakened love to which the mystic passes when his purification is at an end is to him, above all else, the state of Song. He does not "see" the spiritual world: he "hears" it. For him, as for St. Francis of Assisi, it is a "heavenly melody, intolerably sweet."

EVELYN UNDERHILL

This rapture affects the will thus: God touches it with His Sweetness, and then, as a needle touched by the magnet turns to the pole, so the will, attracted by the loadstone of Divine Love, is powerfully drawn, and sinks into a rapture, not of knowledge, but of joy; not of admiration, but of affection; not of theory, but of experience; not of sight, but of fruition.

FRANCIS DE SALES

My understanding was lifted up into heaven, where I saw our Lord God as a lord in his own house, who has called all his dearworthy friends to a grand feast . . . I saw him royally reign in his house, and filling all full of joy and mirth, himself endlessly gladdening and consoling his dearworthy friends, humbly and courteously, with a marvelous melody of endless love, his own fair blessed face glorious, a cheer which fills all heaven with joy and bliss.

JULIAN OF NORWICH

For the soul mixes with the wine of God's love the milk of natural affection, that is, the desire for her body and its glorification. She glows with the wine of holy love which she has drunk; but she is not yet all on fire, for she has tempered the potency of that wine with milk. The unmingled wine would enrapture the soul and make her wholly unconscious of self; but here is no such transport for she is still desirous of her body. When that desire is appeased, when the one lack is supplied, what should hinder her then from yielding herself utterly to God, losing her own likeness and being made like unto him? At last she attains to that chalice of the heavenly wisdom, of which it is written, "My cup shall be full." Now indeed she is refreshed with the abundance of the house of God, where all selfish, worrisome care is done away, and where, for ever safe, she drinks the fruit of the vine, new and pure, with Christ in the Kingdom of His Father.

BERNARD OF CLAIRVAUX

Rapture leaves behind a certain strange detachment also, which I shall never be able to describe; I think I can say that it is in some respects different from—yea, higher than—the other graces, which are simply spiritual; for though these effect a complete detachment in spirit from all things, it seems that in this of rapture our Lord would have the body itself to be detached also: and thus a certain singular estrangement from the things of earth is wrought.

TERESA OF ÁVILA

Immensely absorbed in delicate flames, subtly wounded with love through each of them, and more wounded by all of them together, more alive in the love of the life of God, the soul perceives clearly that that love is proper to eternal life.

JOHN OF THE CROSS

It is not what you are, nor what you have been, that God beholds with merciful eyes—but that which you want to be.

ANONYMOUS (*THE CLOUD OF UNKNOWING*)

Now the mystics in all ages have insisted that, whether the process be named "instinct," or "intuition," or "inner sense," or "uprushes," the spirit of man is capable of immediate experience of God. There is something in man, "a soul-center" or "an apex of soul," which directly apprehends God. It is an immense claim, but those who have the experience are as sure that they have found a wider world of life as is the person who thrills with the appreciation of beauty.

RUFUS JONES

Between God and the blissful soul that has become God with God, there reigns a spiritual charity. So whenever God reveals this spiritual charity to the soul, there rises within it a tender friendship. That is, it feels within it how God is its friend before all pain, in all pain, and above all pain, yes, beyond all pain, in fidelity toward his Father.

HADEWIJCH

The purified and illuminated mind, when clearly participating in the grace of God, also beholds other mystical and supernatural visions—for in seeing itself, it sees more than itself: It does not simply contemplate some other object, or simply its own image, but rather the glory impressed on its own image by the grace of God.

GREGORY PALAMAS

Part Three

DIVINIZATION

XXIII.

Monasteries are silent so that the monks may discover—and quietly surrender—the noise within. Contemplatives do not create silence, for silence is already given to us—it is our birthright as children of a loving God. To enter mystical silence involves not doing something, but doing *less*—less attachment to the chatter within, the endless commentary spun by the thinking mind. Between and beneath all our thoughts, our daydreams, our interior imagination, rests vast, open, limitless silence. It's always there. We simply need to learn to notice the silence, and in noticing it, to touch it. To touch that silence is to enter the presence of God.

For God alone my soul waits in silence,
for my hope is from him.

PSALM 62:5

In mystical silence, as Rumi often calls it, there is a phase in which the mystics so leave themselves behind that it is no longer they who speak their prayer but God in them. The experience of infused prayer testifies to a silence in which God is as active as the human being.

DOROTHEE SOELLE

God is that goodness which may not be wrathful, for God is naught but goodness. Our soul is "oned" with God, the unchangeable goodness. Not even wrath or God's forgiveness can come between us. For our soul is so fully "oned" with God, of his own goodness, that between God and our soul there is truly nothing.

JULIAN OF NORWICH

This universal consolation of Christ will, perchance, be found to descend preferably upon those who await their Lord in peaceful silence; on those who are in affliction; on those who are poor and detached from the world.

BERNARD OF CLAIRVAUX

The Father spoke one Word, which was his Son, and this Word he speaks always in eternal silence, and in silence must it be heard by the soul.

JOHN OF THE CROSS

The grace in your heart shall guide you when to speak and when to remain still. It shall govern you discretely, without error in all aspects of your life, and teach you mystically how to begin and cease all your natural activities, with a great and sovereign discernment.

ANONYMOUS (THE EPISTLE OF DISCRETION)

Love needs no language, but it does express itself in perfect silence.

GEORGE A. MALONEY

Trinity! . . . lead us beyond all knowledge and light, to the highest summit of your mystic Word, where your simple, absolute, and changeless mysteries rest hidden in the luminous darkness of your silence.

DIONYSIUS THE AREOPAGITE

There is very great virtue in the cultivation of silence, and strength to be found in using it as a door to God. Such a door opens within. When I have quieted down, I must spend some time in self-examination in the Presence of God. This is no facile admission of guilt for wrongs done or a too quick labeling of attitudes in negative terms. But it does mean lifting up a part of one's self and turning it over and over, viewing it from many angles and then holding it still as one waits for the movement of God's spirit in judgment, in honesty and in understanding.

HOWARD THURMAN

There are times when good words are to be left unsaid out of esteem for silence.

BENEDICT OF NURSIA

Speak only when your words are an improvement on silence.

QUAKER PROVERB

The water of your doctrine flows in silence. Your teaching is not poured into hearts by an eloquent tongue but breathed into hearts by your sweet spirit. Of you it is written: His voice will not strain or shout. It will not be heard abroad. Inside it is heard; within the heart it is heard; in silence it is heard.

PRAYER OF AELRED OF RIEVAULX

XXIV.

The mystical life is not hostile to reason, yet it calls us to a place beyond the limits of the intellect. While it would be a mistake to call it *ir*rational or *pre*-rational, a more appropriate way to describe mystical knowing is *trans*-rational. Some of the greatest mystics were profound philosophers, yet like Thomas Aquinas, they came to see that their discursive knowledge was like only so much straw, when compared to the deeper knowing that takes us beyond the limitations of thought, of grammar, of syntax, of logic. Contemplative unknowing is a higher knowing, a knowing of the heart. It is ineffable. It is infinite.

Then his disciples asked Jesus what this parable meant. He said, "To you it has been given to know the mysteries of the kingdom of God; but to others I speak in parables, so that 'looking they may not perceive, and listening they may not understand.'"

LUKE 8:9-10

The contemplative act, which is an act of loving and self-forgetting concentration upon the Divine—the outpouring of man's little and finite personality towards the Absolute Personality of God—will, in so far as it transcends thought, mean darkness for the intellect; but it may mean radiance for the heart. Psychologically, it will mean the necessary depletion of the surface-consciousness, the stilling of the mechanism of thought, in the interests of another center of consciousness.

EVELYN UNDERHILL

All must be done with a simplicity of heart entirely founded on love, keeping yourself with Our Lord as a little child with its father: and when it happens that you commit faults, whatever they may be, ask Our Lord's pardon for them very quietly, saying to him that you are well assured he loves you dearly and will pardon you: and this always simply and sweetly.

FRANCIS DE SALES

Many mysteries are privately hidden, which may never be known, until the time that God of his goodness makes us worthy to see.

JULIAN OF NORWICH

Seek the surer knowledge of faith, which discerns truths unknown to the senses, beyond the range of experience.

BERNARD OF CLAIRVAUX

I am not now asking you to meditate on Him, nor to produce great thoughts, nor to feel deep devotion: I only ask you to look at Him. Who can prevent your turning the eyes of your soul (but for an instant, if you can do no more) on our Lord?

TERESA OF ÁVILA

That you may know everything, seek to know nothing.

JOHN OF THE CROSS

Lift up your heart to God with a meek stirring of love, seeking God, and not any of God's works or blessings. See to it that you think of nothing but God, so that nothing acts within your wits or your will but God.

ANONYMOUS (THE CLOUD OF UNKNOWING)

What great truths are hidden even from Christians who imagine themselves most enlightened!

JEAN-PIERRE DE CAUSSADE

Yet the characteristic of the divine nature is to transcend all characteristics. Therefore, he who thinks God is something to be known does not have life, because he has turned from true Being to what he considers by sense perception to have being. . . . True Being is true life. This Being is inaccessible to knowledge.

GREGORY OF NYSSA

If I wish to write on a white tablet, whatever else is written on the tablet, however noble its purport, is a hindrance to me. If I am to write, I must wipe the tablet clean of everything, and the tablet is most suitable for my purpose when it is blank. Similarly, if God is to write on my heart, everything else must come out of it till it is really sanctified.

MEISTER ECKHART

XXV.

If you are holding something in your hand, you won't be able to pick up anything else. First you have to set down whatever it is you're holding, and then you're free to grasp the new item. That's common sense, but it applies equally well to the spiritual life.

A cup must be empty before it may be filled. A mind must release its anxious grasp on cherished beliefs in order to be open to learning something new. A heart must be empty of our transitory attachments in order to receive the wine of divine love.

Whether it is a matter of renunciation or indifference, non-attachment always makes liberation possible.

So if you have been raised with Christ, seek the things that are above, where Christ is, seated at the right hand of God. Set your minds on things that are above, not on things that are on earth, for you have died, and your life is hidden with Christ in God.

COLOSSIANS 3:1-3

The Poverty of the mystics, then, is a mental rather than a material state. Detachment of the will from all desire of possessions is the inner reality, of which Franciscan poverty is a sacrament to the world. It is the poor in spirit, not the poor in substance, who are to be spiritually blessed.

EVELYN UNDERHILL

[When you pray], make yourself therefore quite indifferent as to whether you get what you ask or not, and cease not still to ask with confidence. Remain in indifference as to having or not having spiritual goods: and when you feel that you lack confidence to approach Our Lord, on account of the multitude of your imperfections, then bring into play the superior part of your soul, saying words of confidence and love to him, with the greatest fervor and frequency you can.

FRANCIS DE SALES

Our Lord did not say, "You shall not be tempest-tossed, you shall not be travailed, you shall not be distressed"—he said, "You will not be overcome." God wills that we take heed of this word, that we be ever mighty in secure trust, in wellness and in woe. For he loves us and likes us, and so God wills that we love him and like him and mightily trust in him, and all shall be well.

JULIAN OF NORWICH

The soul can no more be satisfied by earthly treasures than the hunger of the body can be satisfied by air. If you should see a starving man standing with mouth open to the wind, inhaling draughts of air in hope this would gratify his hunger, you would think him a lunatic. But it is no less foolish to imagine that the soul can be satisfied with worldly things which only inflate it without feeding it.

BERNARD OF CLAIRVAUX

He who cares nothing for the good things of the world has dominion over them all.

TERESA OF ÁVILA

All the sweetness and all the pleasures which all the things of this world furnish to the will are, in comparison with the sweetness and pleasure which is God, supreme pain, torment, and bitterness.

JOHN OF THE CROSS

A good will (directed toward God in love) is the substance of all perfection. All sweetnesses and comforts, whether physical or spiritual, be they ever so holy, are incidental to this good will, and can exist only because of our good will; I say "incidental" because they can be present or absent in a person's life without adversely affecting our will.

ANONYMOUS (*THE CLOUD OF UNKNOWING*)

The soul that discerns the will of God in the smallest event, even when it is the most distressing, receives all things with an equal joy, pleasure, and respect.

JEAN-PIERRE DE CAUSSADE

The Little Book of Christian Mysticism

Were we to have the tiniest glimpse of God, we would lose desire for anything else.

RUTH BURROWS

The character of emptiness, at least for a Christian contemplative, is pure love, pure freedom. Love that is free of everything, not determined by any thing, or held down by any special relationship. It is love for love's sake.

Thomas Merton

XXVI.

No word can capture God, no image may depict God, no concept may define God. All our human efforts to express the ineffable ultimately fail. Indeed, it has been a truism of mystical wisdom that we ultimately cannot say anything definitive about God at all: we cannot say what God *is*, we are only capable of saying what is *not* God. No wonder that images of darkness, of unknowing, of hiddenness, of mystery, of the night and nothing, remain so common in the writings of the great mystics and contemplatives.

This does not need to be a problem, even if some may find it disorienting. God, the hidden God, the unknown God, invites us into the mystery, invites us to step out in faith. To the extent that we can trust the mystery and respond to its invitation, we may find a well of unending bliss.

Take delight in the Lord,

. . . and he will give you the desires of your heart.

PSALM 37:4

Contemplation is an act of love, the wooing, not the critical study, of Divine Reality. It is an eager outpouring of ourselves towards a Somewhat Other for which we feel a passion of desire; a seeking, touching, and tasting, not a considering and analyzing, of the beautiful and true wherever found. It is, as it were, a responsive act of the organism to those Supernal Powers without, which touch and stir it.

EVELYN UNDERHILL

In a word, meditation is the mother of love, but contemplation is the daughter; and consequently I call contemplation a loving attention.

FRANCIS DE SALES

In all this time, from the beginning to the end, I had two manner of beholding. One was endless, continuous love, with security of keeping and blissful salvation. For all of my showings were about this. The other was the common teaching of Holy Church, in which I had been previously formed and grounded, and which shaped my life and my understanding.

Julian of Norwich

We need first of all compunction of heart, then fervor of spirit; thirdly, the labor of penance; fourthly, works of charity; fifthly, zeal for prayer; sixthly, leisure for contemplation; seventhly, love in all its fullness.

Bernard of Clairvaux

What we behold with faith, the soul here (as one may say) understands by sight, though this sight is not with the eyes of the body, because it is not an imaginary vision.

TERESA OF ÁVILA

Faith, which is obscure night, illumines the soul which is in darkness, according to the words of the Psalmist, "Night shall be my light in my pleasures," (Psalm 139:11) that is, in the pleasures of pure contemplation and of union with God. The night of faith shall guide me. The soul, therefore, must be in darkness that it may have light, and be able to journey on the spiritual road.

JOHN OF THE CROSS

The one who desires to see God must cleanse his soul, which is like a mirror which reflects all things clearly, when it is clean . . . Therefore cleanse your mirror, and light your candle by the fire, so that when it is cleansed, and burning, you may utterly behold the first glimmers of the clear light of God, which will shine in your soul, like a spiritual sunbeam that appears before your spiritual sight, which opens the eye of your soul to behold God and godly things, heaven and heavenly things, and all manner of spiritual things.

ANONYMOUS (*THE STUDY OF WISDOM*)

We become contemplatives when God discovers Himself in us.

THOMAS MERTON

Stand in the path of the vision you have chosen. Cleanse the eyes of your heart so that you may raise them in contemplation of the light in which life dwells, which is your redemption.

ELISABETH OF SCHÖNAU

Stand guard over your spirit, keeping it free of concepts at the time of prayer so that it may remain in its own deep calm.

EVAGRIUS PONTICUS

XXVII.

One of the most primal fears is the fear of death. Most day-to-day fears—whether the fear of failure, or of embarrassment, or of criticism or ridicule—ultimately are simply the fear of not being able to handle whatever it is life throws our way. But the fear of death is a category all its own. Even for a person of faith, death is the ultimate mystery, the final silence, the passage from which there is no real return.

Susan Jeffers, PhD once wrote a book with the title *Feel the Fear and Do It Anyway*. We overcome our fears, paradoxically, when we enter into them. We discover that spiders, or snakes, or clowns, lose their power to terrify when we slowly approach them and desensitize our reptilian resistance to them.

Likewise, the only true antidote to the fear of death is to die, spiritually if not physically. Those who are spiritually prepared to die often find that they leave the fear behind, and approach their final days or hours with a serene calm.

Even before that final day when we surrender our spirit to God, we are invited, perhaps many times over a lifetime, to die spiritually: to die to self. Such a dying is the only gateway to the most intimate mysteries. We die to self, to live to God.

I have been crucified with Christ; and it is no longer I who live, but it is Christ who lives in me. And the life I now live in the flesh I live by faith in the Son of God, who loved me and gave himself for me.

GALATIANS 2:19-20

The detachment of the mystic is just a restoration to the liberty in which the soul was made: it is a state of joyous humility in which he cries, "Nought I am, nought I have, nought I lack." To have arrived at this is to have escaped from the tyranny of selfhood: to be initiated into the purer air of that universe which knows but one rule of action—that which was laid down once for all by St. Augustine when he said, in the most memorable and misquoted of epigrams: "Love, and do what you like."

EVELYN UNDERHILL

As to cure diseases of the skin it is not so necessary to wash or bathe the body as it is to purify the blood and strengthen the liver; so to cure our vices, although it may be good to mortify the flesh, yet it is, above all, necessary to purify our affections, and to refresh our hearts effectually. But in and through all, let us be sure never to undertake corporal austerities, but with the advice of our spiritual guide.

FRANCIS DE SALES

In this life we have, in us, a marvelous medley both of wellness and of woe. We have, in us, our risen Lord Jesus Christ, and we also have in us the wretchedness and the mischief of Adam's falling. Dying, we will be everlastingly kept by Christ, and by his gracious touch we are raised into the secure trust of salvation.

JULIAN OF NORWICH

Love the Lord your God with the full and deep affection of your heart, love him with your mind wholly awake and discreet, love him with all your strength, so much so that you would not even fear to die for love of him.

BERNARD OF CLAIRVAUX

If we have really begun to serve our Lord, the least we can offer Him is our life, after having yielded our will to Him. What is there to fear in this?

TERESA OF ÁVILA

If the soul had but one single glimpse of the grandeur and beauty of God, it would not only desire to die once in order to behold Him, but would endure joyfully a thousand most bitter deaths to behold Him even for a moment, and having seen Him would suffer as many deaths again to see Him for another moment.

JOHN OF THE CROSS

For in the love of Jesus shall be your help. Love is so powerful that it makes all things common. Love Jesus, and all he has is yours.

Anonymous (The Cloud of Unknowing)

I tell you that not only your true self but the very Word of God is coming to birth in you. That is why you can cry out with Paul, "It is no longer I that live but Christ lives in me." That is why you can say with Paul, "For me to live is Christ . . ." You are becoming more and more filled with the presence of one who loves you and gave himself up for you.

William Johnston

Yes, let us be one with God even in this life; and for this we should be more than resigned, we should embrace the Cross with joy.

Thérèse of Lisieux

If God is definitively to enter into us, he must in some way hollow us out, empty us, so as to make room for himself. And if we are to be assimilated into him, he must first break down the molecules of our being so as to recast and remould us.

PIERRE TEILHARD DE CHARDIN

XXVIII.

Letting go is painful. There is something innately human about wanting to grasp what we have, to hoard our treasures, to hold on tightly to the person we do not want to leave.

But as difficult as it may be to let go, once we have opened our hands and surrender to what is asked of us, we can find peace. Letting go is painful, but *to have let go* is freedom.

The mystic enters the dark night of the soul to let go of everything. To let go of not only all our earthly attachments, but even all the inner and spiritual "things" we grasp. The dark night is an unrelenting master, and demands of us complete surrender. Then, even the darkness itself must be surrendered.

God said to Elijah, "Go out and stand on the mountain
before the Lord, for the Lord is about to pass by."
Now there was a great wind,
so strong that it was splitting mountains and breaking
rocks in pieces before the Lord,
but the Lord was not in the wind;
and after the wind an earthquake,
but the Lord was not in the earthquake;
and after the earthquake a fire,
but the Lord was not in the fire;
and after the fire a sound of sheer silence.

I KINGS 19:11-12

The Little Book of Christian Mysticism

The Dark Night, then, is really a deeply human process, in which the self which thought itself so spiritual, so firmly established upon the supersensual plane, is forced to turn back, to leave the Light, and pick up those qualities which it had left behind. Only thus, by the transmutation of the whole man, not by a careful and departmental cultivation of that which we like to call his "spiritual" side, can Divine Humanity be formed: and the formation of Divine Humanity—the remaking of man "according to the pattern showed him in the mount"—is the mystic's only certain ladder to the Real.

EVELYN UNDERHILL

Darkness and solitude of night are delightful to me, on account of God's all-presence, which we may enjoy better in this solitude.

FRANCIS DE SALES

Our faith is a light, kindly coming of our endless day that is our father, God; in this light our mother, Christ, and our good Lord, the Holy Spirit, leads us in this passing life. This light is measured discreetly, standing with us even in the night.

JULIAN OF NORWICH

Joy is most welcome after sadness, rest after toil, harbor after shipwreck. Everyone enjoys security, but no-one so much as one who has known fear. Light is pleasant to everyone, but particularly to someone who has escaped from the tyranny of darkness. To have passed from death to life doubles the beauty of life.

BERNARD OF CLAIRVAUX

God guides those He loves by the way of afflictions; the dearer they are to Him, the more severe are their trials. It is incredible that He should hate contemplatives whom He Himself praises and calls His friends, and absurd to imagine that He would admit self-indulgent and easy-going people into His friendship; I feel certain that God gives by far the heaviest crosses to His favorites.

TERESA OF ÁVILA

He who will walk in the way of perfection must not only enter through the narrow gate, emptying himself of everything that relates to sense, but must also renounce all that he possesses, laying a constraint upon himself, and releasing himself entirely from all attachment even to spiritual things.

JOHN OF THE CROSS

The higher part of contemplation, to the extent it may be had here on earth, suspends us entirely in darkness and the cloud of unknowing, where with a loving impulse we behold, darkly, the naked being of God, and God alone.

ANONYMOUS (THE CLOUD OF UNKNOWING)

Moses' vision of God began with light (Exodus 19.18); afterwards God spoke to him in a cloud (Exodus 20.21). But when Moses rose higher and became more perfect, he saw God in the darkness (Exodus 24.15-18).

GREGORY OF NYSSA

Cross and night are the way to heavenly light: that is the joyful message of the cross.

EDITH STEIN

The dark night is a profoundly good thing. It is an ongoing spiritual process in which we are liberated from attachments and compulsions and empowered to live and love more freely.

GERALD G. MAY

XXIX.

An elderly Trappist monk once told me, "Everyone is not called to be a mystic, but everyone is called to holiness." I disagree with him about the call to be a mystic—but I do agree with him about holiness. In the Catholic tradition we speak of "the universal call to holiness." Holiness is not just for saints or monks or nuns, it's for everyone. And if we say everyone is called to be a mystic, then it only stands to reason that everyone is equally called to be holy.

If mystics cultivate intimacy with God, holiness is how they share that intimacy with others. The two great commandments, according to Christ, are to love God, and to love our fellow human beings (our "neighbors"). Mysticism is the expression of our love for God; holiness is the expression of our love for neighbors. They belong together, and each requires the other. To be a mystic means being—or at least becoming—holy. No one is perfect, but all are called to walk the path.

Anyone united to the Lord becomes one spirit with him.

I CORINTHIANS 6:17

But the union here set up between man and God, between the finite and infinite life, is incomplete so long as it remains the union of the "Alone with the Alone." Divine Love is not a single thread that links creature and Creator; but rather a web that knits up the many with the One.

EVELYN UNDERHILL

Learn to measure all virtues by obedience to love, loving each virtue for itself, but chiefly because it is acceptable to God, and preferring that which is best, not because it is best, but because God loves it best.

FRANCIS DE SALES

Our faith is a virtue that comes of our kind substance into our sensual soul by the Holy Spirit, in which virtue all our virtues come to us. For without that, no one may receive virtue. For it is naught else but a right understanding with true belief and secure trust of our being, that we are in God and God in us, even though we do not see it.

JULIAN OF NORWICH

We surely do not suppose that we have therefore comprehended the mysteries of God. It is not reason that comprehends them, but holiness, if it is possible to comprehend that which is incomprehensible! But unless such comprehension were possible, the Apostle would not have said, "That we may comprehend with all Saints." The Saints, therefore, comprehend. Do you ask how? If you are holy you have comprehended, and know; if you are not, then become holy and you shall know firsthand. Holy affection makes a person holy, and that is a twofold affection: the holy fear of the Lord, and holy love. When the soul is perfectly possessed by these, it comprehends as if clasping God with two arms—embraces, draws close, holds tight, and says, "I have held Him fast, and will not let Him go."

BERNARD OF CLAIRVAUX

Desire only the will of God; let us place ourselves in His hands, for He loves us exceedingly, and we cannot do wrong if with a determined will we persevere herein.

Teresa of Ávila

The Spirit of God, while hidden in the veins of the soul, is sweet water quenching its spiritual thirst; but when the soul offers the sacrifice of love the Spirit is then living flames of fire, and these are the lamps of the acts of love.

John of the Cross

God does not want your help; God only wants you. God wills only that you look upon him, and then leave him to act alone.

Anonymous (*The Cloud of Unknowing*)

Philosophers are not only those that contemplate happiness, but practice virtue.

THOMAS TRAHERNE

Our duty therefore in our present state, and the employment of our whole lives, must be constantly and fervently to coöperate with divine grace, . . . to beget and increase divine love in us; and a continual uninterrupted union in spirit with God, by faith contemplating Him, and by love ever adhering to Him.

AUGUSTINE BAKER

Let your mouth constantly speak words of blessing; then the scorn of another will never hurt you. Disdain gives birth to disdain, blessing to blessing.

ISAAC THE SYRIAN

XXX.

"This is my body," said Jesus; "this is my blood." Ever since that dramatic night just hours before his death, Jesus's commandment to partake in communion through his body and blood has remained a central ritual act for Christians.

"When we eat this Bread and drink this Cup, we proclaim your Death, O Lord, until you come again." But we not only *proclaim* Christ's death, resurrection, and eventual return—we *participate* in it.

After all, nutritionists like to remind us: "You are what you eat."

Communion is a "union with"—a mystical embrace where lover and lover remain distinct to love, yet become one with love. It's not just something that happens with bread and wine: there is such a thing as a *spiritual* communion, as well. The wisdom of the mystics calls us into this place of ever-deepening union with Love, in love. Here we approach the heart of the mystery.

Christ has given us . . . his precious and very great promises, so that through them you . . . may become participants of the divine nature.

II PETER 1:2-4

Even that mysterious communion with God in which we seek, and offer ourselves to, that which we love—in spite of the deep peace it brings—is not without the pain and tension which must be felt by imperfect human creatures, when they contemplate and stretch towards a beauty and perfection which they cannot reach. Still more when it comes to the deeper action, the more entire self-giving, the secret transformation to which that vision of perfection calls us; and the sacrifice, struggle and effort which, sooner or later, this transformation must involve. The Perfection at which the awakened soul gazes is a magnet, drawing him towards itself. It means effort, faithfulness, courage, and sometimes grim encounters if he is to respond to that attraction, and move towards it along the narrow track which leads up and out from the dark valleys of the mind.

EVELYN UNDERHILL

O my God, when Thy Gracious Presence fills man's heart with sweet perfumes, sweeter far than honey and wine, then every faculty of his soul is hushed in a grateful repose, lulled so utterly to rest, that no power save that of the will is awake, and that is unconsciously absorbed in the inconceivable bliss of its Present God!

FRANCIS DE SALES

For the fullness of joy is to behold God in all: for by the same blessed Might, Wisdom, and Love, that He made all things, to the same end our good Lord leads it continually, and therefore Himself shall bring it; and when it is time we shall see it.

JULIAN OF NORWICH

God is love, and the deeper one's union with God, the more full one is of love.

BERNARD OF CLAIRVAUX

Whenever you receive Holy Communion beg some gift from God for the sake of His great mercy in visiting your poor soul.

TERESA OF ÁVILA

Moses said, "The Lord your God is a consuming fire" (Deuteronomy 4:24). In other words, God is a fire of love. Since His power is infinite, God consumes infinitely, burning with great power, and transforming into Himself all that He touches.

JOHN OF THE CROSS

You have no business now except to make sure that your dark contemplation of the substance of your being be lifted up in gladness and loving desire to be joined and made one in grace and in spirit with the precious being of God just as he is in himself, and nothing more.

ANONYMOUS (*THE LETTER OF PRIVATE DIRECTION*)

The Little Book of Christian Mysticism

While I am here, He is in me; after this life, I am in Him. All things are therefore possible to me, if I am united to Him Who can do all things.

MEISTER ECKHART

Union with God is neither acquired nor received; it is *realized*, and in that sense it is something that can be yearned for, sought after, and—with God's grace—found.

GERALD G. MAY

The world serves you in ways that transcend the imagination. If it only sustained your body, preserved your life and comforted your senses, you would be bound to value it accordingly; but it reveals the very being of God to you. It opens His nature, and shows you His wisdom, goodness and power, it magnifies His love for you, it serves angels and mortals for you, it entertains you with many lovely and glorious objects, it feeds you with joys, and furnishes you with themes for perpetual praise and thanksgiving to God. If you so choose, it will enflame you with the love of God, and serve as the foundation for your union and communion with God. Our world is the temple in which you are exalted to glory and honor before God, and it is the visible porch or gate of Eternity—a sure pledge of Eternal joys, to all who walk before God and thus are perfect within it.

THOMAS TRAHERNE

XXXI.

In the western branch of Christianity—the traditions of Roman Catholicism, Protestantism, and Evangelicalism—we speak of the spiritual life as leading us toward *sanctification*: being made holy. Eastern Christianity, however, has preserved and remembered an earlier truth: that God calls us not merely into ever-increasing goodness, but truly to embody *theosis*—what the mystics call Union with God. This is not pantheism—to be deified is not to be made equal with God, but to be enclosed within the fullness of divine love and felicity. Think of it rather like a drop of water participating in the ocean, or of a drop of water poured into a chalice of wine—the wine is greater than the water, and the water loses itself into the wine. This is the splendor of a life lived in response to the love of God: the mystical life.

"I ask not only on behalf of these, but also on behalf of those who will believe in me through their word, that they may all be one. As you, Father, are in me and I am in you, may they also be in us, so that the world may believe that you have sent me. The glory that you have given me I have given them, so that they may be one, as we are one, I in them and you in me, that they may become completely one, so that the world may know that you have sent me and have loved them even as you have loved me."

JESUS (JOHN 17:20-23)

The completed mystical life, then, is more than intuitional: it is theopathetic. In the old, frank language of the mystics, it is the deified life . . . Such a word as "deification" is not, of course, a scientific term. It is a metaphor, an artistic expression which tries to hint at a transcendent fact utterly beyond the powers of human understanding, and therefore without equivalent in human speech: that fact of which Dante perceived the "shadowy preface" when he saw the saints as petals of the Sempiternal Rose. Since we know not the Being of God, the mere statement that a soul is transformed in Him may convey to us an ecstatic suggestion, but will never give exact information: except of course to those rare selves who have experienced these supernal states.

EVELYN UNDERHILL

Be the soul's union with God conscious or unconscious, He is alike its Author, and none can approach or attain Him "except the Father draw him:" "Draw me, we will run after Thee." Now the perfection of this union lies in two points—purity and strength. If I approach any one in order to speak to him, to see him, to obtain somewhat of him, or lean upon him, I certainly draw near, but my main object is not so much union with him, as to promote whatever may be my immediate object. But if I approach with no other end in view than to enjoy his immediate presence, this is simply and purely to seek union with him.

FRANCIS DE SALES

Prayer unites the soul to God. For though the soul be ever like God in kind and substance, restored by grace, it is often unlike God in Condition, because of our sin. Thus, prayer is a witness that the soul wills as God wills; prayer comforts the conscience and enables us to receive grace.

And thus God teaches us to pray, and to trust mightily that we shall have union with God. For He beholds us in love and wants to make us partners of His good deed, and therefore He stirs us to pray for that which it pleases him to do.

JULIAN OF NORWICH

You have seen the way that we must follow, the order of procedure: first, we cast ourselves at his feet, we weep before the Lord who made us, deploring the evil we have done. Then we reach out for the hand that will lift us up, that will steady our trembling knees. And finally, when we shall have obtained these favors through many prayers and tears, we humbly dare to raise our eyes to his mouth, so divinely beautiful, not merely to gaze upon it, but I say it with fear and trembling—to receive its kiss. "Christ the Lord is a Spirit before our face," and he who is joined to him in a holy kiss becomes through his good pleasure, one spirit with him.

BERNARD OF CLAIRVAUX

Remember what St. Augustine tells us . . . how he sought God in many places and at last found the Almighty within himself.

TERESA OF ÁVILA

The greater the faith of the soul the more is that soul united to God.

JOHN OF THE CROSS

God is a spirit, and whosoever wishes to be one with God needs to align with the truth found deep within the spirit, far removed from the duplicity of the body. Everything is known to God and nothing can be hidden from God, whether physical or spiritual. Therefore, it is best to be authentic and open with God, sharing all that is hidden deep in your spirit with God.

ANONYMOUS (*THE CLOUD OF UNKNOWING*)

The grace of salvation, the grace of Christian wholeness that flowers in silence, dispels this illusion of separation. For when the mind is brought to stillness, and all our strategies of acquisition have dropped, a deeper truth presents itself: we are and have always been one with God and we are all one in God (John 17:21).

MARTIN LAIRD

Christian life consists not so much in being good as in becoming God. The Holy Spirit's work in us goes beyond the reformation of our morals. It is a matter of forming us so that we become sharers in the divine nature and, because of this, capable of fulfilling the impossible demands that the New Testament imposes upon us.

MICHAEL CASEY

Let us rise up, at last, since the Scripture excites us when it says, "it is already time for you to awaken out of sleep!" And having opened our eyes to the deifying light, let us hear with awestruck ears how the divine voice daily admonishes us, saying: "Today, oh that you would hear his voice! Don't harden your heart!"

BENEDICT OF NURSIA

XXXII.

A Trappist monk once told me that he didn't like the concept of "the Beatific Vision." He believed that the joy we will find after heaven involves more than just being a spectator looking at some unchanging perfection. "I believe our destiny is a *Beatifying Communion*," he said.

The mystical life leads to an ever-opening blossom of union and communion, a dance of love and compassion. The end is not some static state, devoid of change and energy and life; rather, it is a celebration of eternally expanding transfiguration and joy. The dance goes on forever, and the circle grows ever wider.

Jesus took with him Peter and James and his brother John and led them up a high mountain, by themselves. And he was transfigured before them, and his face shone like the sun, and his clothes became dazzling white. Suddenly there appeared to them Moses and Elijah, talking with him. Then Peter said to Jesus, "Lord, it is good for us to be here; if you wish, I will make three dwellings here, one for you, one for Moses, and one for Elijah." While he was still speaking, suddenly a bright cloud overshadowed them, and from the cloud a voice said, "This is my Son, the Beloved; with him I am well pleased; listen to him!" When the disciples heard this, they fell to the ground and were overcome by fear. But Jesus came and touched them, saying, "Get up and do not be afraid." And when they looked up, they saw no one except Jesus himself alone.

As they were coming down the mountain, Jesus ordered them, "Tell no one about the vision until after the Son of Man has been raised from the dead."

MATTHEW 17:1-9

So, what is being offered to you is not merely a choice amongst new states of consciousness, new emotional experiences— though these are indeed involved in it—but, above all else, a larger and intenser life, a career, a total consecration to the interests of the Real. This life shall not be abstract and dreamy, made up, as some imagine, of negations. It shall be violently practical and affirmative; giving scope for a limitless activity of will, heart, and mind working within the rhythms of the Divine Idea. It shall cost much, making perpetual demands on your loyalty, trust, and self-sacrifice: proving now the need and the worth of that training in renunciation which was forced on you at the beginning of your interior life.

EVELYN UNDERHILL

And oh! what bliss will it be to see the Face of God, the one paramount desire of the soul! Our heart is athirst, and cannot be quenched with mortal joy, which if moderate does not satisfy, if immoderate chokes us . . . as the famished babe cleaves to its mother's breast as though it would fain absorb it, so our panting soul cleaves to God as though to be for ever absorbed in Him, and He in us!

FRANCIS DE SALES

And suddenly, as I beheld Christ on the cross, his face changed into blissful cheer. The changing of his face changed mine, and I became all glad and merry, as possible as could be. And merrily our Lord spoke into my mind, "Is there any point to your pain or your grief?" And so, I was filled with merry joy.

JULIAN OF NORWICH

The Little Book of Christian Mysticism

As a drop of water poured into wine loses itself, and takes the color and savor of wine; or as a bar of iron, heated red-hot, becomes like fire itself, forgetting its own nature; or as the air, radiant with sun-beams, seems not so much to be illuminated as to be light itself; so in the saints all human affections melt away by some unspeakable transmutation into the will of God. For how could God be all in all, if anything merely human remained in man? The substance will endure, but in another beauty, a higher power, a greater glory.

BERNARD OF CLAIRVAUX

The soul sometimes leaps forth out of itself, like a fire that is burning and is become a flame; and occasionally this fire increases violently—the flame ascends high above the fire; but it is not therefore a different thing: it is still the same flame of the same fire.

TERESA OF ÁVILA

Love never reaches perfection until the lovers are so alike that one is transfigured in the other.

JOHN OF THE CROSS

Your words are few, but full of fruit and fire. A brief word that you speak contains a whole world of wisdom, yet it seems mere foolishness to those who remain in their senses. Your silence is sweet, your speech most profitable, your prayers are secret, your pride most guiltless, your behavior is humble, your cheerfulness mild, your delight is pleasure in playing with a child.

ANONYMOUS (*THE BOOK OF PRIVY COUNSELING*)

We must try everything for Christ; we must hope everything for Christ. *Nihil intentatum* (leave nothing untried). That, on the contrary, is the true Christian attitude. To divinize does not mean to destroy, but to sur-create. We shall never know all that the Incarnation still expects of the world's potentialities. We shall never put enough hope in the growing unity of mankind.

PIERRE TEILHARD DE CHARDIN

For the soul's sense is love; by love it perceives whatever it perceives; alike when it is pleased and when it is offended. When the soul reaches out in love to anything, a certain change takes place in it by which it is transmuted into the object loved; it does not become of the same nature as that object, but by its affection it is conformed to what it loves.

WILLIAM OF ST. THIERRY

The eye with which I see God is exactly the same eye with which God sees me. My eye and God's eye are one eye, one seeing, one knowledge and one love.

MEISTER ECKHART

XXXIII.

"All you need is love." The Beatles may have said it, but the Christian mystics live it.

In the end, it's all about love. Union with God is union with Love. We gaze into the eyes of Love, and the eyes of Love gaze back, and it is one gaze. We dance into the arms of Love, and Love leads the dance, and the dancers form one dance. We know the heart of Love, and Love knows us, and it is one knowing.

Alleluia. Amen.

Beloved, let us love one another, because love is from God; everyone who loves is born of God and knows God. Whoever does not love does not know God, for God is love. God's love was revealed among us in this way: God sent his only Son into the world so that we might live through him. In this is love, not that we loved God but that he loved us and sent his Son to be the atoning sacrifice for our sins. Beloved, since God loved us so much, we also ought to love one another. No one has ever seen God; if we love one another, God lives in us, and his love is perfected in us.

By this we know that we abide in him and he in us, because he has given us of his Spirit. And we have seen and do testify that the Father has sent his Son as the Savior of the world. God abides in those who confess that Jesus is the Son of God, and they abide in God. So we have known and believe the love that God has for us.

God is love, and those who abide in love abide in God, and God abides in them. Love has been perfected among us in this: that we may have boldness on the day of judgment, because as he is, so are we in this world. There is no fear in love, but perfect love casts out fear; for fear has to do with punishment, and whoever fears has not reached perfection in love. We love because he first loved us.

I JOHN 4:7-19

The wheel of life has made its circle. Here, at the last point of its revolution, the extremes of sublimity and simplicity are seen to meet. It has swept the soul of the mystic through periods of alternate stress and glory; tending ever to greater transcendence, greater freedom, closer contact with "the Supplier of true life." He emerges from that long and wondrous journey to find himself, in rest and in work, a little child upon the bosom of the Father. In that most dear relation all feeling, will, and thought attain their end. Here all the teasing complications of our separated selfhood are transcended. Hence the eager striving, the sharp vision, are not wanted any more. In that mysterious death of selfhood on the summits which is the medium of Eternal Life, heights meet the deeps: supreme achievement and complete humility are one.

In a last brief vision, a glimpse as overpowering to our common minds as Dante's final intuition of reality to his exalted and courageous soul, we see the triumphing spirit, sent out before us, the best that earth can offer, stoop and strip herself of the insignia of wisdom and power. Achieving the highest, she takes the lowest place. Initiated into the atmosphere of Eternity, united with the Absolute, possessed at last of the fullness of Its life, the soul, self-naughted becomes as a little child: for of such is the kingdom of heaven.

EVELYN UNDERHILL

Love is a bond, "the bond of perfectness," and he who loves most is most closely bound to God. And by this I do not mean the habitual, permanent union which exists whether we sleep or wake, but of that active union which is the result and utterance of love.

FRANCIS DE SALES

Before God made us, God loved us. This love has never been quenched, and never will be. In the love God has done all of his work, and in this love God has made all things profitable to us. And in this love our life is everlasting. Because God created us, we have a beginning; but the love in which God created us has no beginning . . . All this we shall see in God, without end.

JULIAN OF NORWICH

Love, the law of the Lord, joins the Father, Son and Holy Spirit into the unity of the Godhead and unites the holy Trinity in the bond of peace . . . It is the very substance of the Godhead; and my assertion is neither novel nor extraordinary, since St John says, "God is love." One may therefore say with truth that love is at once God and the gift of God, essential love imparting the quality of love. Where the word refers to the Giver, it is the name of His very being; where the gift is meant, it is the name of a quality. Love is the eternal law whereby the universe was created and is ruled.

BERNARD OF CLAIRVAUX

Let us realize, my daughters, that true perfection consists in the love of God and of our neighbor, and the more nearly perfect is our observance of these two commandments, the nearer to perfection we shall be.

TERESA OF ÁVILA

All my occupation now is the practice of love for God, all the powers of soul and body, memory, intellect, and will, interior and exterior senses, the desires of the spiritual and of the sensitive nature, all work in and by love. All I do is done in love; all I suffer, I suffer in the sweetness of love.

JOHN OF THE CROSS

God loves without limit and this puts a loving person most securely at peace.

JOHN RUUSBROEC

Whosoever would enjoy the happiness of Paradise must put on the charity of Paradise.

THOMAS TRAHERNE

What we, as believers, call love is at the most a poor likeness of that which God calls love. For this reason, God has disclosed to us his own love, and faith teaches us, not just to see this love, but to live in it.

ADRIENNE VON SPEYR

Read the authentic mystics and you will find them saying: "Mysticism is love. No love: no mysticism." So be sure that human love penetrates your life and that it keeps growing and growing. No need to tell you that there are many kinds of love, and that all play a crucial role in your life of prayer.

WILLIAM JOHNSTON

FOR then, perfectly fulfilled in us, will be the prayer of our Saviour in which He prayed for His disciples to the Father, saying "that the love with which you have loved me may be in them, and I in them;" and again: "that they may all be one, as you, Father, are in me and I am in you, may they also be in us," when that perfect love of God, in which "He first loved us" has come into our hearts as well, in fulfilment of this prayer of Jesus which cannot possibly be ineffectual. And this will come to pass when God shall be all our love, and every desire and wish and effort, every thought of ours, and all our life and words and breath, and that unity which already exists between the Father and the Son, and the Son and the Father, has been poured into our hearts and minds, so that as He loves us with a pure and unfeigned and indissoluble love, so we also may be joined to Him by a lasting and inseparable affection, since we are so united to Him that whatever we breathe or think, or speak *is* God... This then ought to be the destination of the solitary, this should be all his aim that it may be vouchsafed to him to possess even in the body an image of future bliss, and that he may begin in this world to have a foretaste of that celestial life and glory. This, I say, is the end of all perfection, that the mind purged from all gross desires may daily be lifted towards spiritual things, until the whole life and all the thoughts of the heart become one continuous prayer.

JOHN CASSIAN

EPILOGUE

Thank you for sharing with me these words of wisdom from sacred scripture and from the great saints and mystics of our Christian tradition. This is, of course, a mere sampling of the two millennia's worth of insight and inspiration that has been preserved for us from the hands of the great lovers of God, both past and present.

It's important to remember, however, that mysticism is not a kind of spiritual museum. We have only one important reason to honor the great mystics of the past: so that we might apply their teachings to our lives here and now, and in the mystery of the present moment, respond to the invitation to embody the Love of God, as it is needed in our time. By doing this, we carry the precious gem of Christian mysticism from the past into the future.

May we all respond joyfully to this living call.

Acknowledgments

Unless marked otherwise, scripture quotations are from the New Revised Standard Version of the Bible, © 1989, Division of Christian Education of the National Council of the Churches of Christ in the United States of America. Used by permission. All rights reserved.

Many of the books used to gather the quotations collected here are part of the Christian Classics Ethereal Library (*www.ccel.org*). CCEL is a marvelous source of online editions of public domain texts, available for anyone to use. Since these books were written or translated many years ago, I have edited many of the quotations to modernize spelling and grammar.

Special thanks to Faithlife Corporation, producers of Verbum Software, which is a Catholic Bible Study Program—and many texts of mystical classics are available for use on the Verbum platform, which makes it an invaluable tool not only for studying the Bible, or getting to know the mystics, but also discovering the many links between Biblical wisdom and the teachings of the mystics.

Thanks to Fran McColman, Greg Brandenburgh, Linda Roghaar, Linda Mitchell, Brother Elias Marechal, OCSO, and Paco Ambrosetti, for encouragement, support, and kindness.

Notes

1   Unless marked otherwise, all scripture quotations are taken from the New Revised Standard Version (NRSV) of the Bible.

2   All quotations marked "Anonymous" come from the same medieval English mystic, who was probably a fourteenth-century Carthusian monk. This author's best known work is *The Cloud of Unknowing*. Other titles from the same hand include *The Book of Privy Counseling*, *The Epistle of Discretion* and *The Letter of Private Direction*.

3   This is a new translation for this book. This verse gets rendered many different ways, and almost none of the versions make much sense. Most timid modern translations have Jesus using "healthy" and "unhealthy" to describe the eyes. But the original Greek words from the text, ἁπλοῦς and πονηρός, mean "single" and "wicked" respectively.

Reading this from a contemplative/mystical perspective, Jesus appears to be drawing a distinction between seeing non-dually (singly), and seeing dualistically (judgmentally, i.e., looking for something wicked to judge). .

FOR FURTHER READING

Anonymous. *The Cloud of Unknowing and Other Works*.

Augustine of Hippo. *The Confessions*.

Benedict of Nursia. *The Rule of Saint Benedict*.

Bernard of Clairvaux. *Sermons on the Song of Songs*.

The Bible, New Revised Standard Version.

Brother Lawrence of the Resurrection. *Practice of the Presence of God*.

Burrows, Ruth. *Guidelines for Mystical Prayer*.

Casey, Michael. *Fully Human, Fully Divine*.

Cassian, John. *The Conferences*.

De Caussade, Jean-Pierre. *Abandonment to Divine Providence*.

De Sales, Francis. *Introduction to the Devout Life*.

Dionysius the Areopagite. *Works*.

Eckhart, Meister. *The Sermons*.

Egan, Harvey, ed. *An Anthology of Christian Mysticism*.

Evagrius Ponticus. *The Praktikos & Chapters on Prayer*.

John of the Cross. *Collected Works*.

Julian of Norwich. *Revelations of Divine Love.*

Laird, Martin. *Into the Silent Land.*

Marechal, Elias. *Tears of an Innocent God.*

McColman, Carl. *Answering the Contemplative Call.*

McColman, Carl. *The Big Book of Christian Mysticism.*

McColman, Carl. *Christian Mystics.*

McGinn, Bernard. *Essential Writings of Christian Mysticism.*

Merton, Thomas. *Contemplative Prayer.*

Merton, Thomas. *New Seeds of Contemplation.*

Reinhold, H. A. *The Soul Afire: Revelations of the Mystics.*

Rohr, Richard. *The Naked Now.*

Ruusbroec, John. *Spiritual Espousals.*

Teilhard de Chardin, Pierre. *The Divine Milieu.*

Teresa of Ávila. *The Complete Works* (three volumes).

Thérèse of Lisieux. *The Story of a Soul.*

Thurman, Howard. *Meditations of the Heart.*

Underhill, Evelyn. *Practical Mysticism.*

Underhill, Evelyn. *The Spiritual Life.*

BIBLIOGRAPHY

Aelred of Rievaulx. *For Christ Luve: Prayers of S. Aelred Abbot of Rievaulx*. Martinus Nijhoff, 1965.

Angela of Foligno. *The Complete Works*. Paulist Press, 1993.

Anonymous. *The Cloud of Unknowing and Other Works*. Penguin Books, 2001.

Anonymous. *The Cloud of Unknowing and Related Treatises*. Catholic Records Press, 1982.

Anonymous. *The Cloud of Unknowing and the Book of Privy Counseling*. Image Books, 1973.

Anonymous. *The Pursuit of Wisdom and Other Works*. Paulist Press, 1988.

Arrupe, Pedro. *Essential Writings*. Orbis Books, 2004.

Arrupe, Pedro. *In Him Alone is Our Hope*. Irish Messenger Publications, 1983.

Augustine of Hippo. *The Confessions*. Logos Research Systems, Inc., 1996.

Baker, Augustine. *Holy Wisdom*. Burns Gates & Washbourne Ltd., 1876.

Beatrice of Nazareth, "There Are Seven Manners of Loving" (13th century), from *Medieval Women's Visionary Literature*. Oxford University Press, 1986.

Benedict of Nursia, *The Rule of Saint Benedict*. Liturgical Press, 1981.

Bernard of Clairvaux. *The Letters*. Burns & Oates, 1958.

Bernard of Clairvaux. *The Life and Works of Saint Bernard*. Aeterna Press, 2004.

Bernard of Clairvaux. *Magnificat: Homilies in Praise of the Blessed Virgin Mary*. Burns & Oates, 1979.

Bernard of Clairvaux. *On Consideration*. Clarendon Press, 1908.

Bernard of Clairvaux. *On Loving God*. CCEL, N.D.

Bernard of Clairvaux. *Selected Works*. Paulist Press, 1987.

Bernard of Clairvaux. *Sermons on Advent & Christmas*. Benziger Brothers, 1909.

Bernard of Clairvaux. *Sermons on the Song of Songs*. Four Volumes. Cistercian Publications, 1971–1980.

The Bible, New Revised Standard Version. Oxford University Press, 1989.

Bonaventure. *Mystical Opuscula*. St. Anthony Guild Press, 1960.

Brother Lawrence of the Resurrection. *Practice of the Presence of God*. ICS Publications, 1994.

Burrows, Ruth. *Guidelines for Mystical Prayer*. Dimension Books, 1976.

Casey, Michael. *Fully Human, Fully Divine*. Liguori Publications, 2004.

Catez, Elizabeth (of the Trinity). *The Complete Works of Elizabeth of the Trinity, Volume 2*. ICS Publications, 1995.

Catherine of Genoa. *Purgation and Purgatory; The Spiritual Dialogue*. Paulist Press, 1979.

Catherine of Siena. *The Dialogue of the Seraphic Virgin*. Kegan Paul, Trench, Trübner & Co., 1896.

De Caussade, Jean-Pierre. *Abandonment to Divine Providence*. Herder, 1921.

De Caussade, Jean-Pierre. *Abandonment to Divine Providence*. Image Books, 1975.

De Caussade, Jean-Pierre. *Inner Peace*. Pauline Books, 2011.

De Chantal, Jane Frances. *Selected Letters*. R & T Washbourne, Ltd., 1918.

De Sales, Francis. *Introduction to the Devout Life*. M. H. Gill & Son, 1885.

De Sales, Francis. *Letters to Persons in Religion*. Benziger Brothers, 1909.

De Sales, Francis. *Of the Love of God*. Rivingtons, 1888.

De Sales, Francis. *Practical Piety Set Forth by Saint Francis de Sales*. Burns and Lambert, 1851.

De Sales, Francis. *The Spiritual Conferences*. Benziger Brothers, 1909.

De Sales, Francis & Jane de Chantal. *Letters of Spiritual Direction*. Paulist Press, 1988.

Dionysius the Areopagite. *Works*. James Parker & Co. 1897.

Eckhart, Meister. *Selected Writings*. Penguin Books, 1994.

Eckhart, Meister. *The Sermons of Meister Eckhart*. Allenson, N.D.

Egan, Harvey, ed. *An Anthology of Christian Mysticism*. Liturgical Press, 1996.

Elisabeth of Schönau. *The Complete Works*. Paulist Press, 2000.

Evagrius Ponticus. *The Mind's Long Journey to the Holy Trinity*. Liturgical Press, 1993.

Evagrius Ponticus. *The Praktikos & Chapters on Prayer*. Cistercian Publications, 1981.

Gertrude the Great of Helfta. *The Spiritual Exercises*. Cistercian Publications, 1989.

Gibran, Kahlil. *The Prophet*. Knopf, 1923.

Gregory of Nyssa. *From Glory to Glory*. Scribners, 1961.

Gregory of Nyssa. *The Life of Moses*. Paulist Press, 1978.

Guerric of Igny. *Liturgical Sermons, Volume I*. Cistercian
Publications, 1970.

Hadewijch. *The Complete Works*. Paulist Press, 1980.

Harmless, William. *Desert Christians*. Oxford University Press,
2004.

Houselander, Caryll. *The Reed of God*. Ave Maria Press, 2006.

Ignatius of Loyola. *Spiritual Exercises*. Loyola Press, 1992.

Isaac of Ninevah (Isaac the Syrian). *Mystical Treatises*. Akademie
Van Wetenschappen, 1923.

Isaac the Syrian. *The Ascetical Homilies*. Holy Transfiguration
Monastery, 2011.

John of the Cross. *Ascent of Mount Carmel*. Thomas Baker, 1906.

John of the Cross. *Collected Works*. ICS Publications, 1991.

John of the Cross. *Complete Works* (two volumes). Longman,
1864.

John of the Cross. *The Dark Night of the Soul*. Newman Press,
1935.

Johnston, William. *Being In Love*. Fount, 1989.

Jones, Rufus. *The Inner Life*. Macmillan, 1917.

Julian of Norwich. *Revelations of Divine Love*. Methuen & Co.,
1911.

Julian of Norwich. *The Writings of Julian of Norwich*. Pennsylvania
State University Press, 2006.

Laird, Martin. *Into the Silent Land*. Oxford University Press, 2006.

Leseur, Elisabeth. *Selected Writings*. Paulist Press, 2005.

MacDonald, George. *Unspoken Sermons, Series I*. Alexander Strahan, 1867.

Maloney, George. *Inward Stillness*. Dimension Books, 1976.

Marechal, Elias. *Tears of an Innocent God*. Paulist Press, 2015.

Matarasso, Pauline, ed. *The Cistercian World: Monastic Writings from the Twelfth Century*. Penguin Books, 2006.

Maximus Confessor. *Selected Writings*. Paulist Press, 1985.

May, Gerald G. *The Dark Night of the Soul*. Harper Collins, 2004.

Mechthild of Magdeburg. *Flowing Light of the Godhead*. Paulist Press, 1998.

Merton, Thomas. *The Asian Journal of Thomas Merton*. New Directions, 1975.

Merton, Thomas. *Conjectures of a Guilty Bystander*. Image Books, 1968.

Merton, Thomas. *Contemplative Prayer*. Image Books, 1971.

Merton, Thomas. *Mystics and Zen Masters*. Farrar, Straus & Giroux, 1967.

Merton, Thomas. *New Seeds of Contemplation*. New Directions, 1962.

Merton, Thomas. *Thoughts in Solitude*. Farrar, Straus & Cudahy, 1958.

Palamas, Gregory. *The Triads*. Paulist Press, 1983.

Reinhold, H. A. *The Soul Afire: Revelations of the Mystics*. Image Books, 1973.

Ruusbroec, John. *The Spiritual Espousals and Other Works*. Paulist Press, 1985.

Ruysbroeck (Ruusbroec), John. *The Seven Steps on the Ladder of Spiritual Love*. Holmes Publishing, 1989.

Stein, Edith. *The Science of the Cross*. ICS Publications, 2011.

Tauler, John. *The Inner Way*. Methuen & Co., 1901.

Teilhard de Chardin, Pierre. *The Divine Milieu*. Harper & Row, 1965.

Teilhard de Chardin, Pierre. *Hymn of the Universe*. Harper & Row, 1961.

Teresa of Ávila. *The Complete Works* (three volumes). Sheed and Ward, 1946.

Teresa of Ávila. *Interior Castle*. T. Jones, 1852.

Teresa of Ávila. *Interior Castle*. Paulist Press, 1979.

Teresa of Ávila. *Interior Castle*. Riverhead Books, 2004.

Teresa of Ávila. *The Life of St. Teresa of Avila*. Thomas Baker, 1916.

Teresa of Ávila. *Minor Works*. Thomas Baker, 1913.

Teresa of Ávila. *Peace in Prayer*. Pauline Books, 2011.

Teresa of Ávila. *The Way of Perfection*. Thomas Baker, 1919.

Thérèse of Lisieux. *The Story of a Soul*. Burns & Oates, 1912.

Thomas Aquinas. *Summa Theologica*. Burns Oates & Washbourne, N.D.

Thurman, Howard. *Jesus and the Disinherited*. Abingdon Press, 1949.

Thurman, Howard. *Meditations of the Heart*. Beacon Press, 1981.

Thurman, Howard. *Mysticism and the Experience of Love*. Pendle Hill Publications, 1961.

Traherne, Thomas. *Centuries of Meditations*. Cosimo Classics, 2007.

Underhill, Evelyn. *Abba*. Longmans, Green & Co., 1940.

Underhill, Evelyn. *The Essentials of Mysticism*. Aeterna Press, 2015.

Underhill, Evelyn. *The Life of the Spirit and the Life of To-Day*. Methuen & Company, 1922.

Underhill, Evelyn. *The Mystery of Sacrifice*. Longmans, Green & Co., 1938.

Underhill, Evelyn. *Mysticism*. E. P. Dutton, 1961.

Underhill, Evelyn. *The Mystic Way*. E. P. Dutton & Co., 1913.

Underhill, Evelyn. *The Mystics of the Church*. James Clarke &
    Co., 1925.

Underhill, Evelyn. *Practical Mysticism*. E. P. Dutton, 1915.

Underhill, Evelyn. *The Spiritual Life*. Harper & Brothers, 1937.

von Speyr, Adrienne. *The Boundless God*. Ignatius Press, 2004.

Whichcote, Benjamin. "The Joy Which the Righteous Have in
    God" (1650), from *Cambridge Platonist Spirituality*. Paulist
    Press, 2004.

William of St. Thierry. *On Contemplating God; Prayer; Meditations*.
    Cistercian Publications, 1977.

Hampton Roads Publishing Company

. . . for the evolving human spirit

Hampton Roads Publishing Company publishes books on a variety of subjects, including spirituality, health, and other related topics.

For a copy of our latest trade catalog, call (978) 465-0504 or visit our distributor's website at *www.redwheelweiser.com*. You can also sign up for our newsletter and special offers by going to *www.redwheelweiser.com/newsletter/*.